the quilter's
appliqué
workshop

the quilter's
appliqué
workshop

TIMELESS TECHNIQUES FOR MODERN DESIGNS

Kevin Kosbab

INTERWEAVE
interweave.com

To my mom,
master appliqué artist
and inspiration.

EDITOR Michelle Bredeson

TECHNICAL EDITOR Linda Turner Griepentrog

ASSOCIATE ART DIRECTOR / DESIGNER Julia Boyles

LAYOUT DESIGNER Dean Olson

ILLUSTRATOR Missy Shepler

PHOTOGRAPHER Joe Hancock

PHOTO STYLIST Allie Liebgott

PRODUCTION DESIGNER Katherine Jackson

Interweave
A division of F+W Media, Inc.
201 East Fourth Street
Loveland, CO 80537
interweave.com

Manufactured in China by RR Donnelley Shenzhen.

Library of Congress Cataloging-in-Publication Data

Kosbab, Kevin
The quilter's appliqué workshop : timeless
techniques for modern designs / Kevin Kosbab.

pages cm

Includes index.

ISBN 978-1-59668-861-2 (pbk)
ISBN 978-1-59668-897-1 (PDF)

1. Patchwork--Patterns. 2. Quilting--Patterns. 3.
Appliqué--Patterns.

I. Title.

TT835.K6668 2014

746.46--dc23

2013026350

10 9 8 7 6 5 4 3 2 1

contents

INTRODUCTION
give appliqué a chance

When I first discovered appliqué, I felt like the possibilities of quiltmaking were suddenly infinite. No longer limited to the straight edges (and a few tricky curves) of piecing, I could incorporate any shape I liked into a quilt through the miracle of appliqué. I started with circles in a conventional quilt-block grid, but it wasn't long before I was appliquéing a huge flamingo across the pieced background of a full-size quilt. As soon as I tried appliqué, I knew it was for me, and I dove right in.

When I started quilting (and appliquéing), I lived in a big city, without a car to get me to a quilt shop or guild, and there wasn't nearly as much quilting information on the Internet then as there is today. So between a few general quiltmaking books and phone calls to my appliqué-expert mother, I figured out the basics of hand and machine appliqué. She showed me needle-turn appliqué one Christmas, and then I was hooked for good.

The reason I mention my appliqué education is this: If I can essentially teach myself to appliqué within a year of starting to quilt, with no home-ec training or other "official" sewing background, it can't be that hard. In fact, my newbie sewing status may well have helped me—I had no idea so many quilters consider appliqué to be the dreaded "A-word," so I didn't know there was anything to be scared of. Years later, I still maintain that appliqué isn't a difficult process and that anyone can do it with some practice.

Many people fall in love with appliqué. Spend any time in quilt guilds, and you'll encounter a spectrum of firm positions regarding appliqué, the most extreme of which being those who consider piecing a chore that must done to join appliqué blocks and those who would rather never make another quilt than appliqué a single block. The appliqué enthusiasts, though, are sometimes drowned out by the A-word crowd. You may have heard these old chestnuts from them, but I've got an appliqué-loving response for 'em all.

IT'S TOO *hard.*
Anything is difficult if you haven't learned how to do it. For most hand appliqué, there's really only one stitch to learn, and it isn't very complicated. I promise there's no magic involved.

IT TAKES TOO *long.*
It's true that appliqué isn't as quick as motoring through some chain-pieced blocks on your machine, but not every appliqué project has to be an elaborate Baltimore Album masterpiece—start small, practice, and build your confidence.

I DON'T HAVE THE *patience.*
Sewing by hand can be extremely soothing (I suspect this is partly why antidepressants weren't invented until people stopped doing needlework as a matter of course). These days, I don't have the patience to watch TV without a stitching project at hand.

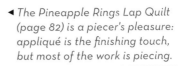

◄ *The Pineapple Rings Lap Quilt (page 82) is a piecer's pleasure: appliqué is the finishing touch, but most of the work is piecing.*

IT'S TOO *fussy.*

There are plenty of appliqué patterns with dauntingly tiny pieces, but that's a style rather than a definition of the technique itself. The two biggest quilts in this book—Cobblestones (page 48) and Counterbalance (page 88)—are some of the quickest to sew thanks to concentrated areas of appliqué and large shapes, respectively. You don't have to deal with fiddly little bits until you're ready. Once you're at that point, the challenge of teeny appliqué can be rewarding rather than daunting.

I HATE *sewing by hand.*

Don't worry; there's lots of appliqué you can do by machine. Some things are just easier to stitch by hand, so it pays to make friends with a hand needle, but you can certainly manage without.

I'VE TRIED, AND IT ALWAYS *looks sloppy.*

Nobody's perfect at first, but if you've had bad luck with one appliqué method, try another. If you're perplexed by needle-turn appliqué, try a prepared-edge technique so your shapes are all set before you start sewing. Or give one of my improvisational projects a try—it's easier to loosen up mentally when the project doesn't require precision.

I truly think appliqué is fun and, for the most part, easy. If you're interested at all in making quilts, I really encourage you to expand your options by giving appliqué a try. And if you've already embraced appliqué, I hope you'll find a few tricks and new ideas in these pages, too!

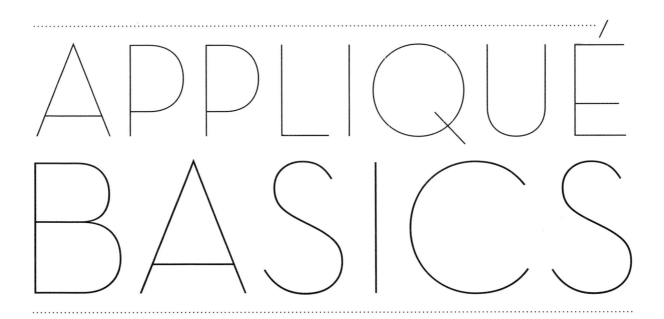

APPLIQUÉ BASICS

If you've made pieced quilts, you'll already have many of the supplies and skills you need to venture into the wide world of appliqué. You can get up to speed on all the essential tools, materials, and techniques right here.

choosing an appliqué method

I approach technique as a means to an end: the more techniques I'm comfortable with, the more tools I have to execute the design ideas floating around my head. Appliqué is a category of techniques rather than a one-size-fits-all process, and each method has particular practical and aesthetic advantages.

By definition, *appliqué* is the application of one fabric onto another, comparable to collage. The fabrics may be glued together or stitched, though this book deals only with sewn appliqué—fusibles and glue are used, but only to hold the appliqué in place until it's sewn. The three main chapters of the book correspond to three main ways of applying one fabric to another: *raw-edge*, in which the edges of the appliqué pieces are not turned under; *prepared-edge*, in which the edges are turned under prior to sewing; and *needle-turn*, in which the edges are turned under as you sew the pieces to the base. Many quilting guidebooks, instead, categorize appliqué methods as either hand- or machine-sewn, but some preparation methods are used interchangeably for hand and machine sewing. All three parts of this book include hand-sewn projects, and only the needle-turn chapter doesn't include a machine-sewn project, since the sewing and turning are integrated with this method.

Still, choosing between hand or machine work is one of the first things you'll want to decide for a project. I always opt for machine appliqué when I know a project is going to get a lot of wear—picnic blankets, children's quilts, and that sort of thing. Machine appliqué is also faster than by hand, but keep in mind that it isn't necessarily speedy: it takes time and concentration to keep the needle accurately positioned along appliqué edges.

The differences in how appliqué techniques look when finished are worth considering, too. I don't consider raw-edge zigzag-stitched appliqué interchangeable with invisible machine appliqué, for example, because the raw-edge zigzags remain visible. Even with a closely matching thread color, the stitching still creates an outline around the shape, which may be just what you're looking for. I've made owl eyes with a fused circle of black fabric, zigzagged with heavy yellow thread to make an iris; in this case, the stitching actually contributed to the appliqué. But invisible machine appliqué, on the other hand, can give a nicely rounded edge to felt snowmen.

Even techniques that appear similar have slight differences. A finished block of starch-turned prepared-edge appliqué looks flatter than needle-turn, because all the shapes have been pressed around freezer-paper templates. I like to use starch-turn for large shapes with crisp, curved edges, such as the circles in the Pineapple Rings Lap Quilt (page 82) and the bulb-like shapes of the

Converting Patterns

Most appliqué patterns come with instructions for one method of appliqué. If that's not the method you want to use, patterns can usually be adapted to another. You'll just need to know whether the pattern is already reversed or not and whether it needs to be reversed for your desired method—I include an "At a Glance" box at the beginning of each part of the book to help with that. You may need to modify some shapes to suit your method, for example, if converting a fusible raw-edge pattern with narrow slits into a technique that requires a seam allowance.

Improvising with Appliqué

Throughout the book, I'll encourage you to embrace imprecision. Appliqué is so often seen as something that requires absolutely accurate reproduction of a pattern, but to me that sort of perfectionism seems at odds with the very nature of handwork. Even when you're sewing by machine, you're not a machine yourself, and your quilts don't have to look like they rolled off an assembly line. While I'm not trying to encourage sloppy craftsmanship, I do think it can be helpful when learning appliqué to not hold yourself to the standards of robotic precision—shapes of flowers and fruits vary in nature, so why not in appliqué?

One of the projects in each section of the book is especially designed to encourage this sort of "improvisational" appliqué, in which the pattern is a starting place rather than an ultimate goal—all of the main appliqué methods lend themselves to different sorts of improvisational approaches. Some of these projects include patterns with suggested shapes and sizes, but I recommend allowing yourself to play directly with the fabric and see what happens. You can make an exact copy of my sample if you want, but I'm really hoping to give you the tools and ideas to express your own creativity.

From top to bottom: ▶
Raw-edge appliqué (Mod Flowers Table Runner, page 44), prepared-edge appliqué (Pineapple Rings Lap Quilt, page 82), needle-turn appliqué (Fruit Market Quilt, page 132).

Counterbalance Quilt (page 88). Many die-hard appliqué enthusiasts swear by the same method for complex blocks with lots of tiny overlapping shapes, but I find I can control the shape of the fabric better with a needle than I can with an iron. When it comes down to it, I just prefer the process: the prep for needle-turn appliqué is relatively minimal, and then I can watch the finished shapes emerge as I sew the edges. Starching the edges doesn't excite me, and then when the block's glued up, it looks like it will when finished, so there's no gradual reveal.

But that's just me—and that's the point. I encourage you to play a little with each technique to see what you feel most comfortable with. Practice makes perfect with any method, so as you work, you'll probably find your skills developing along with the technique you like best. It's helpful to know more than one option so you can pick and choose, but that choice is completely up to you. Throughout this book, I tell you what works best for me and what I think is generally a good starting place for other people trying appliqué, and the projects use the techniques I think are most appropriate. But by no means do I think my way is the One True Way. What feels natural to me might feel totally awkward to you, and what your machine does beautifully may give my machine the mechanical equivalent of a heart attack. Please don't take my guidelines as absolute. Besides, I'm not standing over your shoulder as you sew, so I'll never know if you do what I say or not!

tools and materials

Each of the appliqué methods detailed later in the book has its own sets of required and nice-to-have tools and supplies, so this section is an overview of everything you'll use to appliqué.

FABRIC

For making quilts, medium-weight woven cotton fabric is ideal. All yardage guidelines in this book assume you're using 45" (114.5 cm) wide quilting cotton unless otherwise specified. I like to mix solids, basic small-scale prints, and large-scale focal prints. A "Choosing Fabric" sidebar accompanies each project and discusses fabric choices in more detail.

Appliqué projects involve two categories of fabric: a background fabric and appliqué fabrics that will be stitched to the background.

The background should be at least as sturdy as the appliqués; this usually isn't a concern when using quilting cottons for both. Even among fabrics designed for quiltmaking, some ravel more than others; be cautious when using these for either background or appliqué. (Background fabrics can be cut slightly larger than necessary to allow some fraying while working the appliqué; pinking or zigzagging the edges will further reduce fraying. Trim oversized backgrounds to the size indicated in the instructions before piecing to any other sections.) Poplin-weight quilting cottons are more tightly woven, fray less, and are a good choice for appliqué shapes that have sharp points or other fiddly areas.

Many quilters insist on prewashing their fabrics to preshrink them and prevent later

Cotton prints range ▶ from subtle to show-stopping, and all have their place in appliqué.

Using—and Making—Scraps

Though several of the projects in this book involve large-scale appliqué shapes, relatively small pieces are more typical of appliqué quilts, making them perfect for using up fabric scraps left from previous projects. Some quilters think of certain techniques as wasteful of fabric; I prefer to think of any "waste" fabric as scraps waiting for appliqué. My Eccentric Concentrics Wall Quilt (page 114), for example, uses excess fabric in the construction—full yards of fabric are used to keep the layers stable while working, even though much is later cut away. I didn't throw out the cut-away fabric; in fact, the white scraps from Eccentric Concentrics ended up as the background squares for the All Seasons Pillows (page 126). I'm especially sure to hold on to scraps of staple fabrics like solids—you never know when they'll come in handy for a tiny appliquéd detail.

I've given some guidance on fabric amounts for the projects in case you are buying yardage, but if you have a healthy scrap stash, you can ignore the yardage requirements for appliqué fabrics and go straight to your scrap basket with patterns or cutting dimensions in hand to see what random bits and pieces you can make use of.

The Mod Flowers Table Runner (page 44) foregoes cotton in favor of felted wool, great for appliqué because the non-fraying edges don't need to be turned under. Even in mainly cotton quilts, very tiny appliqués or those that would be difficult to turn can be made easier by using a little felt or Ultrasuede, like I did for some of the seeds in the Fruit Market Quilt (page 132). The nap of these fabrics can be used advantageously for mouse ears, fluffy snowmen, or anywhere that a contrast texture is desired.

Once you've got the hang of cotton and wool, experiment with other fabrics. Firmly woven silks can be used much like cotton, adding some shine. (Even cottons can have a bit of gloss depending on how they're woven. I used a cotton sateen in my Garden Allotments Quilt [page 120], but I wouldn't recommend it to beginners: the long float threads of sateen and satin weaves fray readily, so proceed with caution!) Fabric collages that aren't necessarily made up into quilts can employ nearly any fiber, with textures such as corduroy and piqué adding a new dimension among glittery lamés and gauzy sheers. Just be aware of the characteristics of each fabric and choose based on the intended end use (and care) of your piece.

color bleeding. I prefer how unwashed fabrics handle—the sizing in the fabric gives them a little stability—so I tend to only pre-wash when I'm suspicious about the quality of the fabric, or when I'm planning to wash the finished project.

THREAD

In addition to piecing thread, you'll need thread to sew your appliqués to the background fabric. I'll discuss my favorites when explaining the appliqué methods, but before that, there's a can of worms that has to be opened. The intricacies of thread size and weight are confusing to say the least, though I'll admit to taking a certain geeky pleasure in deciphering them. Without getting too technical, suffice it to say that "No. 50" or "50-weight" aren't necessarily (but might be) equivalent; they may be labeled on complex technical grounds, or, instead, strictly on the manufacturer's whim, more as an article number. Throughout this book, I've used terms such as "size 50," based on the apparent consensus of manufacturers' labels, to indicate categories of thread size rather than exact weights. I stress that these designations are a handy shorthand rather than a technical absolute. The chart on the opposite page is an overview of the generalized thread sizes used in this book. Counterintuitively, higher numbers mean finer threads; lower numbers are thicker.

Also remember that, for thread at least, size isn't everything: threads made for different purposes are constructed differently. Sewing threads are usually fairly tightly twisted for strength during machine stitching, while embroidery threads have looser twists to better reflect light.

With that out of the way, here are the main groups of threads you'll encounter in this book, along with some good alternatives, with sizes corresponding to the chart on the opposite page.

Cotton Sewing Thread (size 50)

The same stuff you probably use for piecing is also my go-to for raw-edge machine appliqué with a zigzag stitch. Gütermann's cotton sewing thread is quite a bit finer than Mettler's equivalent Silk-Finish thread, so I choose between the two based on how

heavy I want the stitching to look. They're often labeled 50/3 to indicate the thread is made up of three plies.

Fine Machine-Embroidery Cotton (size 60)

This is an ideal bobbin thread when using monofilament thread in the needle, and it can also be used for hand-appliqué methods. I include Mettler Fine Embroidery No. 60 thread in this "size 60" category along with some 2-ply threads described by the manufacturers as 50 weight, such as DMC's Machine Embroidery Thread and Aurifil's 50-weight cotton, and I use all of them interchangeably.

❶ Silk thread; ❷❸ Fine machine-embroidery cotton; ❹ Fine sewing cotton; ❺❻ Cotton sewing threads; ❼ Size 40 quilting cotton; ❽❾ Size 30 machine-embroidery cotton; ❿ Variegated thread; ⓫ Wool thread; ⓬ Rayon machine-embroidery thread; ⓭ Monofilament thread; ⓮ Pearl cotton; ⓯ Size 12 cotton thread; ⓰ Six-strand cotton embroidery floss.

Thread Sizes

SIZE	DESCRIPTION
Size 100	*Very lightweight thread, such as the silk I prefer for hand appliqué.*
Size 60	*Finer (lighter-weight) than regular sewing thread, often called fine machine-embroidery cotton or bobbin thread.*
Size 50	*General-purpose cotton sewing thread. Some variation in actual thread thickness exists between brands.*
Size 40	*Somewhat heavier than regular sewing thread. Often labeled as machine-quilting thread.*
Size 30	*Even heavier, typically labeled as machine-embroidery thread.*
Size 12	*Very heavy thread, probably about the limit of what your machine can handle in the needle, and also suitable for hand embroidery. No. 12 pearl cotton falls into this category.*

All Wound Up

To make perfect machine-appliqué stitches, your thread needs to feed properly based on how it's wound onto the spool. Threads that are stacked—the threads on the spool are all parallel—should be placed on a vertical spool pin. Cross-wound spools—the threads crisscross each other on the spool—feed better on a horizontal spool pin. My machine doesn't have a vertical pin, so for stacked threads, I tape a short dowel rod to the end of my machine and put the thread there.

Silk Thread (size 100)

This extremely fine thread is beautiful, but its main benefit for me is how it virtually disappears when used for hand appliqué. YLI's No. 100 silk thread sews smoothly and is available in a wide range of colors at many quilt shops. To keep the thread from wearing out as you sew, use no more than a 12" to 14" (30.5 to 35.5 cm) length. Heavier silk sewing threads are not suitable for appliqué but can be used for embroidered details.

Monofilament Thread

Used in the needle of your sewing machine, clear or smoke monofilament thread is the key to clear machine appliqué. I prefer polyester to the nylon version. Don't skimp here—no-name brands can feel like fishing line. I use Sulky's invisible monofilament because it's readily available, but quilt shops often stock other reputable brands.

Decorative and Special-Purpose Cotton Threads

These are available in a range of sizes. Size 30 machine-embroidery cotton has a bit of shine and is my favorite for full-looking decorative satin stitches, though I sometimes get away with size 40 machine-quilting thread if that's what I have. Variegated threads change color along their length, which could be an interesting detail around the edge of an appliqué. These are also good threads for prominent quilting—I used a variegated size 30 thread to quilt inside the loops of my Helix Table Topper (page 98).

Rayon Machine-Embroidery Thread

Rayon thread is truly shiny and great for highlighting the edges of machine appliqué. Keep in mind, however, that the thread is designed for decorative purposes, not for structural sewing, and rayon fiber is less resistant to abrasion than cotton. Most commonly available is 40-weight rayon; heavier 30-weight rayon thread can be found, too.

Wool Thread (size 12)

Also aimed at the machine-embroidery market, this thread is a blend of 50% wool and 50% acrylic sold as Lana by Madeira, Genziana, and Aurifil. It's much fluffier than your average sewing thread and a great choice for sewing raw-edge wool appliqué by hand. For machine sewing, use a large needle (size 100/16 to 110/18) and size 50 sewing thread in the bobbin.

Six-Strand Cotton Embroidery Floss

This can be used for hand-appliquéing wool (or raw-edge cotton), using as few or as many strands as you like, depending on how bold you want your stitching to look. Of course, it's also useful for embroidered details of appliqué blocks.

Pearl Cotton

This shiny, non-divisible thread is what I prefer for details on my appliqué, since it makes a more solid line than stranded floss. From heaviest to finest, sizes 3, 5, 8, and 12 are commonly available (though color ranges may be limited in some sizes). Pearl cottons are sold in twisted skeins or wound balls; size 12 cotton thread similar to pearl cotton can also be found on spools for machine (or hand) work.

MARKING TOOLS

Appliqué requires a lot of marking. At the very least, you'll need a light-colored marking tool for dark fabrics and a dark marking tool for light fabrics. These are my favorites, but there are plenty of other marking tools out there to try. And do try first: test any marking tool on a scrap of the fabric you'll be using and make sure it's removable. Quilting cottons are relatively forgiving in this respect, but better to be safe than sorry.

Ceramic-Lead Mechanical Pencil

White ceramic shows up nicely on medium to dark fabrics, stays where you need it, and brushes, erases, or just fades away.

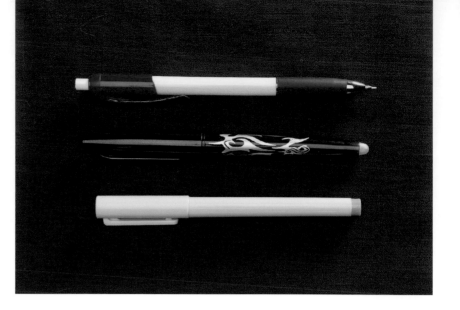

Heat-Removable Pen

Black and other dark colors are best for light fabrics. Marks made on paper by Pilot's FriXion pens can simply be rubbed off; on fabric, an iron does the trick: press your block, and the lines are gone! Some quilters have gone to the trouble of putting their quilts in the freezer to determine that, yes, the opposite of heat does bring the lines back. For needle-turn appliqué, I'm hiding most of my lines anyway, so I'm not overly concerned, but you'll probably want to try another tool for your museum pieces.

Water-Soluble Marker

The familiar blue-ink marker is my main alternative for marking light fabrics. But while a FriXion pen is removed by heat, these markers are set permanently with heat—keep the iron away! Remove the markings by brushing, dabbing, or spraying with water.

Chalk

Available in pencil, roller, and other forms, chalk is best for directly marking on napped fabrics such as felted wool and Ultrasuede. Simply brush it away when the marks are no longer needed.

▲ *Marking tools, from top to bottom: ceramic pencil, FriXion pen, water-soluble marker.*

TRACING TOOLS

Getting appliqué from pattern to fabric requires a few tools, depending on technique.

Freezer Paper

Sold near the aluminum foil and waxed paper at your local supermarket, freezer paper has a million and one uses, and at least half of those relate to quiltmaking. It's essentially a roll of paper coated with plastic on one side: the paper side can be marked with a regular pencil, and the plastic side sticks to fabric when pressed, holding securely in place until peeled away. These properties are perfect for prepared-edge appliqué templates, as well as for transferring needle-turn shapes. Freezer paper cut to letter-sized pages, available at many quilt shops, is convenient for copying onto or inkjet-printing your own designs onto the non-coated side, but don't try feeding it through a laser printer, which uses heat that would make a melty mess.

Paper-Backed Fusible Web

Self-healing mat, clear ▼
acrylic ruler, rotary
cutters, freezer paper,
fabric shears, and
embroidery scissors.

While freezer paper is made with a temporarily bonding plastic, one side of fusible web is coated with an adhesive that permanently bonds fabrics together when pressed. The paper side allows patterns to be traced in pencil before the web is fused to the fabric, then the shape is cut out of both layers. Always fuse according to the manufacturer's instructions, which differ by brand. Lightweight fusible web is used for all the projects in the raw-edge chapter: this type is designed to be sewn through, and though the fusible bond shouldn't be considered removable, fused appliqués may pull away from the design over time if they aren't sewn down.

Light Box

An illuminated surface makes it easier to trace onto dark fabrics or thick materials or to reverse patterns. You can certainly buy a portable light box, but you can also make do by taping a pattern to a sunny window or putting a bright lamp under a glass-topped table or an inverted translucent storage container. My cutting table has a tempered glass inset that I use as a light box because I can (gently) fuse with a craft iron right on top of it. Don't try this on a light box with a plastic top!

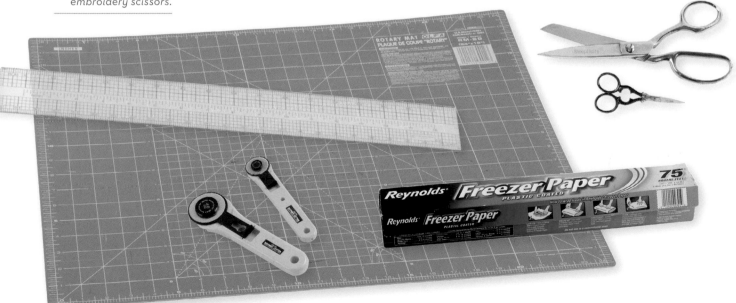

PRESSING TOOLS

An iron and ironing board or other pressing surface is essential for all quilting, and most appliqué methods specifically require them in one way or another.

Iron

The ability to use an iron selectively with and without steam is very helpful; I also like a nonstick sole to keep fusibles at bay. A small craft, hobby, or travel iron is more maneuverable than a full-size laundry iron for prepared-edge appliqué.

Nonstick Pressing Sheet

A pressing sheet keeps fusible adhesives away from your iron or ironing board and is especially useful for raw-edge fusible appliqué, because you can fuse whole sections of overlapped appliqués right on the sheet. Parchment paper meant for cooking has similar nonstick properties and can be used instead of a purpose-made pressing sheet.

CUTTING TOOLS

Long-time sewists tend to accumulate a veritable arsenal of cutting implements. Arm yourself at least with these basics.

Rotary Cutting Tools

A rotary cutter, self-healing mat, and acrylic rulers are quilters' mainstays for cutting rectangular pieces of fabric, including appliqué backgrounds. A 45 mm blade diameter is the most versatile; smaller 28 mm cutters are sometimes suggested for appliqué, but I prefer to cut appliqués with scissors.

Fabric Scissors

Large shears (reserved for fabric use only) make for the smoothest cutting of most appliqué shapes. You'll also want smaller embroidery scissors for snipping threads and cutting into corners—these scissors need to be sharp right up to the tip.

Paper Scissors

Appliqué also requires cutting a lot of paper. A dedicated pair of scissors (not used for fabric) should be used to keep your fabric shears nice and sharp.

BASTING TOOLS

I usually refer to basting an appliqué block as gluing it up, since that's how I do it. You can baste with pins or thread if you prefer, but the instructions all assume you're on board the glue-basting boat.

Basting Glue

This water-soluble, thick liquid glue holds appliqués to the background (and each other) while you're sewing. Small dabs are all that's needed to eliminate the need for pins, which can catch on your sewing thread, fall out, and/or jab you in the hand while you're rummaging through your workbag. I started by glue-basting hand appliqué, but now I use it to hold machine appliqués in place, too—if it isn't fused down, I glue it down. Roxanne Glue-Baste-It is the brand I use; the needle-tip applicator of the bottle makes it easy to direct the glue. Do use the glue sparingly, as big blobs are harder to dissolve.

Appliqué Pins

These are shorter than regular sewing pins, and it's always helpful to have a few on hand to supplement the basting glue. Of course, you can baste entire blocks with pins, but in addition to the disadvantages I noted above, pins can shift, making it more difficult to baste the whole block before you start sewing.

Bent-Arm Safety Pins

Also called curved or quilter's safety pins, they're typically used for basting quilt sandwiches together, they're also handy for holding very large pieces of fabric together temporarily.

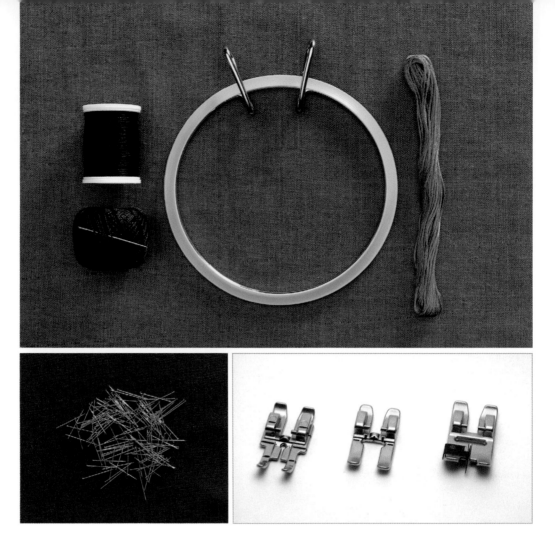

Tools for sewing by hand, ▶
from left to right: heavy
cotton thread (top), pearl
cotton and embroidery
needle (bottom),
embroidery hoop, and
embroidery floss.

Right: Appliqué pins. ▶
Far right: Various presser
feet used for appliqué,
from left to right:
quarter-inch, open-toe,
and narrow-edge.

TOOLS FOR SEWING BY HAND

Beyond the threads suited to a particular appliqué technique, you'll only need a few tools
to complete the actual sewing.

Needles

A No. 11 sharps needle is what I use with silk
thread for almost all of my hand appliqué,
but try several sizes to see whether you're
more comfortable with a longer or shorter
needle (some people prefer a longer milliner's
needle). The Roxanne appliqué needles I like
are slim but sturdy; a thick, bargain needle
can feel like sewing with a nail. Embroidery
needles are better suited to floss, pearl cotton, and wool thread; choose a size that fits
the thread in its eye and pulls easily through
the fabric when threaded.

Thimbles (Optional)

I use one for handquilting but can't seem to
get used to it for appliqué.

Embroidery Hoops

Embroidery hoops are helpful for embroidered details, but I don't use one when sewing the appliqués themselves.

TOOLS FOR SEWING BY MACHINE

You'll need, of course, a sewing machine
for the machine-appliqué methods, but it
doesn't have to be fancy. All the projects in
this book can be done with any machine
that sews a zigzag, though the more control
you have over the characteristics of that
zigzag the better your results will be. See
Sewing Machines for Appliqué (page 20) for
some other worthwhile machine features.
Accessories and other supplies for machine
appliqué are listed on the next page.

Open-Toe Presser Foot

With two projecting toes to hold the fabric down, this foot gives you a clear view of what's under the needle and in its immediate surroundings. You can make do with a standard zigzag foot, but an open-toe foot (sometimes just called an appliqué foot) makes guiding stitches along the edge of your appliqué so much easier.

Narrow-Edge or Edge-Stitch Foot

This one is more optional. A central blade guides your stitching, and depending on the needle position, you can stitch in a ditch or a consistent distance from the blade to either side. I love this foot for topstitching, and I wouldn't stitch in the ditch without it.

Quarter-Inch or "Patchwork" Foot

For piecing appliqué blocks together as well as pre-piecing sections to be appliquéd, this quilters' standby assures a consistent ¼" (6 mm) seam allowance.

Needles

The instructions for appliqué methods will list specific types and sizes of needles where necessary. In general, the best needles for appliqué on quilting cottons have sharp points, such as sharp (or Microtex), embroidery, jeans, and topstitch needles. Choose a size to suit your thread and experiment to see which combinations of thread and needle work best with your particular sewing machine.

Flush Surface Around the Sewing Machine

This isn't crucial but very handy. My sewing machine is in a table with a well that allows the machine arm to sit flush with the table, which lets appliqué blocks lie flat under the machine, rather than falling off the sides of the free arm. Acrylic extension tables are available for a less permanent option.

Sewing Machines for Appliqué

Many quilting books assume you're using a mid- to top-of-the-line, modern sewing machine that's designed with the quilter in mind. While such machines can make work easier in a lot of ways and give you more options, you don't need anything special to make the quilts in this book. My main sewing machine is a secondhand Pfaff from 1986, with a couple electronic features (such as needle-down) but mainly mechanical operations. What people say about not building them like they used to is true in this case—the machine is a workhorse. But it doesn't do some things that would be great for appliqué, such as a blanket stitch or a good blind hem. I've written the appliqué methods so they can be successful on the widest range of machines, but if you're looking for bells and whistles, these are some that make appliqué easier.

- Needle-down function (keeps the needle in the fabric when you stop sewing)
- Fully variable stitch width (not incremental) and needle position
- Good blind-hem stitch (see page 80 for details)
- Good blanket stitch (see page 41 for details)
- Horizontal and vertical spool pins
- Ability to mirror stitches and change stitch density for decorative stitches

By the Numbers

Sewing machines differ in the measurement systems they use for stitch length and width, often labeling them with numbers but no units of measurement (clearly those manufacturers didn't have to do story problems for my third-grade teacher). Millimeters are the most straightforward and often used by European machine companies, but stitches per inch and arbitrary systems also make appearances. I describe all stitch dimensions in this book in millimeters because they are used by many machines (and the most important one—mine!), their small scale is suited to machine stitches, and it's a lot easier to measure a stitch in millimeters than it is to figure out how many stitches of a particular length would fit into 1" (2.5 cm).

basic techniques

These techniques apply throughout the appliqué methods detailed in various chapters. As much as possible, I've kept all instructions hand-neutral: right-handers and lefties will generally work in opposite directions, though whether you work clockwise or counterclockwise around an appliqué is dictated by personal comfort as much as your dominant hand. I'm a righty and sew counterclockwise—you'll know which way feels right to you. Note, though, that the illustrations are drawn from a right-handed perspective.

QUILTMAKING BASICS

This book assumes that you've made a few quilts before and are conversant in basic quiltmaking tasks such as rotary cutting, piecing, pressing, basting, piecing backings, quilting, and binding. By no means do you need to be an expert quilter, but you'll need to have those essentials in your repertoire so we can start adding appliqué to the mix. Some great introductory quiltmaking books are listed in the Resources section if you need a refresher.

Quilt Police, Appliqué Division

Every branch of quilting has its share of self-appointed authoritarians on a mission to ensure compliance with their version of the Right Way to Do Things. Appliqué seems to attract an especially large police force, but as in real law enforcement, their statutes vary by jurisdiction. In some circles, needle-turn is considered the only real appliqué, with all other forms an impure substitute (much as "machine quilting" was once considered a contradiction in terms). The consensus elsewhere is that needle-turn is an old-fashioned, backward method practiced only by those who haven't discovered the joys of freezer paper and starch. Use of glue is a shoot-on-sight offense to other cops. Cotton purists insist the thread fiber match the fabric; the adventurous advance new polyester threads; and then there's the silk-thread camp. I won't even mention fusibles except to say that, all joking aside, there's been at least one scientific study done to assess the effects of time on fusible appliqué—yes, the quilt police make forensic investigations.

All this is to say that, no matter which materials and techniques you choose for your appliqué work, somebody's going to think it's wrong. Just remember that the quilt police are vigilantes—nobody put them in charge. You call the shots for your own work, and you have every right to make the choices that make you happy. Quiltmaking is supposed to be enjoyable!

Most quilt-policing is well-meaning, but the interests and goals of these bossy types may not be yours. I know there are things in my quilts that a quilt judge would frown upon, but I don't make my quilts to enter in shows. I don't imagine the quilts I make today are going to be my taste in fifty years, so if the fusible is a little crusty then, it's not the end of the world. I make quilts because I enjoy making them and enjoy living with them when they're made, not because I want some museum curator in a century to have an easy conservation job. The truth is that most quilts, even if "heirloom quality," are going to be mistreated, abused, or ignored by future generations, and most of them won't have been museum pieces to start with. That may sound depressing, but I think it's actually liberating: quilting for posterity is a daunting task, while making something for you and your loved ones to appreciate now lets you directly delight in the joy that a quilt brings now, today, to yourself and people who mean something to you.

Unless specified, all projects in this book use a ¼" (6 mm) seam allowance. I call for 2" (5 cm) wide binding strips for most of the projects, but you can certainly substitute your preferred width.

TRANSFERRING PATTERNS

For appliqué, most full-size diagrams of the fabric pieces will be a variation on one of two forms: individual shapes or a full schematic of all the shapes put together. I refer to the schematics showing a whole block or other section of appliqué as patterns, and where pieces are shown separately I call them templates. Some designs, such as the Counterbalance Quilt (page 88), needs only templates, and the instructions will tell you how to position the fabric corresponding to them. Others use the pattern as a guide to position multiple pieces of fabric, as in my Fruit Market Quilt (page 132). For projects with a pattern, you'll also trace individual templates of each piece needed from the schematic pattern, usually using a secondary material such as freezer paper or fusible web to transfer the shape to the fabric. (Note that spaces marked with an X are to be cut

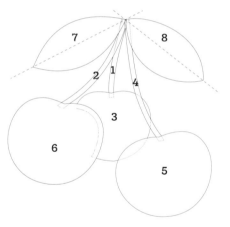

away and are not separate appliqué pieces.) Some appliqué patterns will show you the separate templates as well as the full-size pattern, but it's more common to see just the block patterns, often with lines through the vertical and horizontal center of a block to guide alignment with the background fabric.

Of course, a pattern is just a flat drawing, and your appliqué will usually be layered. If the individual pieces are numbered, piece 1 is the bottommost (i.e., the first one to place on the background); follow the

Broderie perse, as ▶ used in the Garden Allotments Quilt (page 120), dispenses with templates entirely, instead using printed fabric to determine appliqué shapes.

Fussy Cutting

Here I am, trying to say appliqué isn't fussy, and along comes a term like "fussy cutting." It's not really that fussy—it just refers to cutting fabric with regard to where its printed design will fall in the finished shape. You may be familiar with this for piecing—making stripes line up across a seam or fitting a novelty-print animal into a square—but the possibilities for appliqué are even wider. The print details in my China Cupboard appliqués (page 60) were fussy cut, and even the wool felt in the Mod Flowers Table Runner (page 44) was placed with the woven pattern positioned in specific ways to make two-toned leaves from single pieces of wool. I once based an entire quilt design on using an assortment of fussy-cut dots and spots to make the "eyes" on peacock feathers, and I had a blast picking out just the right circular print motifs. Even if you're not using a dominant motif from the fabric, consider the direction of the print for things such as leaves or bird wings—it looks funny if the print runs counter to how the feathers or veins would be in nature. Broderie perse, used for the flowers in my Garden Allotments Quilt (page 120), is really just fussy cutting taken to the extreme: the print dictates the entire shape of the appliqué.

For the fussiest fussy cutting, make a window template by removing the finished pattern shape from a scrap of paper or template material, allowing you to see the exact shape in reference to the printed fabric. But you'll often be able to simply choose a spot by eye before placing your regular template.

numbers sequentially to layer them in the proper order. There are various ways of visually indicating the over- and underlapping pieces on a pattern, and my preferred method is to show lower pieces in full, with the overlapped sections showing as gray lines through the upper piece, as if the upper piece was partially transparent. This way, it's easy to tell what's supposed to go on top.

Each appliqué method has a certain way to transfer pattern shapes to fabric and arrange those shapes on the background fabric; use these general tips as circumstance requires:

▷ Place the pattern on a light box (real or improvised; see page 17); cover with tracing paper, template material (including freezer paper or fusible web), or fabric; and trace individual pieces.

▷ For positioning appliqués, trace the entire pattern onto the background fabric, or simply glue the appliqués in place with the fabric over the pattern on the light box.

▷ To reverse a pattern (refer to the "At a Glance" boxes to see whether you need a reversed pattern or not), place it wrong side up on a light box before tracing. Photocopiers may be able to reverse the pattern too; make sure the original is flat to avoid distortion.

▷ An overlay puts the pattern on top of the fabric rather than underneath: make one by tracing the pattern with permanent pen onto clear vinyl or photocopying onto an overhead transparency. Pin the overlay to the background fabric along one side, aligning the center positions. Slide an appliqué shape under the overlay and guide it into place, then lift the overlay to glue the piece down. Place the overlay back over the fabric and continue positioning pieces in sequence.

EMBROIDERY

Hand embroidery is an excellent complement to appliqué—in fact, appliqué is sometimes considered a form of embroidery. Where you need skinny lines for stems, vines, or anything else, a backstitch or stem stitch does the trick; French knots are perfect for small dots. Other stitches can be used decoratively, too; the All Seasons Pillows (page 126) use appliqué as a backdrop for various stitches.

BACKING

In general, the quilts in this book call for backing fabric that's large enough to give you a 4" (10 cm) margin all the way around the quilt top. In cases where the backing will need to be sewn together to make a single piece large enough to back the quilt, the instructions will tell you whether a horizontal

A sampler of ▶ embroidery stitches form branches on the simple appliqué shapes of the All Seasons Pillows (page 126).

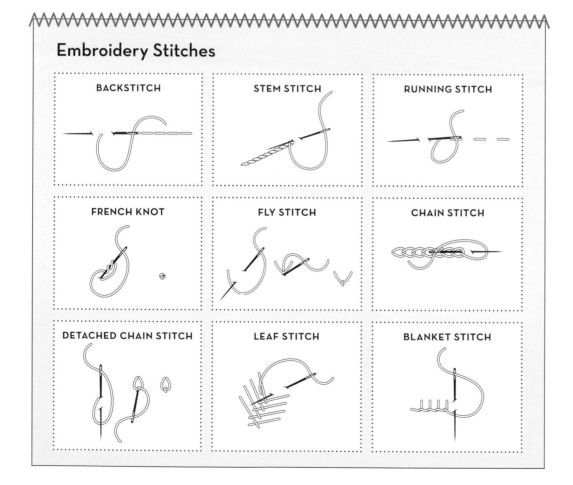

Embroidery Stitches

BACKSTITCH	STEM STITCH	RUNNING STITCH
FRENCH KNOT	FLY STITCH	CHAIN STITCH
DETACHED CHAIN STITCH	LEAF STITCH	BLANKET STITCH

Minding Metrics

The projects in this book were designed using the U.S. system of measurement. The metric conversions that follow the U.S. units are intended for general comparison. Unfortunately for the multinational quilter, converting and rounding is inherently imprecise. You should be fine buying fabric using the meter measures listed, but if you're cutting based on the metric measurements, you may need to adapt the projects so the pieces all fit together properly.

or vertical seam will make most economical use of the fabric. They'll also tell you the minimum size the backing should be, which is useful if you want to piece smaller scraps into a backing or if you're using fabric of a width other than 45" (114.5 cm).

For smaller projects such as table runners and wall quilts, the 45" (114.5 cm) width of

the backing fabric may be a bit shy of the 4" (10 cm) margin, but the small overall size makes a large margin less necessary. I don't know about you, but I'll always back in one piece if I can manage it!

QUILTING APPLIQUÉ QUILTS

All but two of the projects in this book were quilted on my domestic sewing machine—the Fruit Market Quilt (page 132) and Round the Block Kid's Quilt (page 54) were quilted on a long-arm machine, and they're not even the biggest quilts in the book. I quilted so many of these quilts myself because I wanted this book to show that it could be done and hopefully to encourage you to try quilting your own quilts. Ideally, I like to plan fabrics, piecing, appliqué, and quilting to all relate to each other and make sense together, and the best way to do this is to do it all myself.

The main thing that makes quilting appliqué quilts different from their pieced cousins is that appliqué has a slight dimensional quality. All-over quilting patterns that look great on pieced quilts can flatten and obliterate the appliqué. There may be times this would be okay, but usually appliqué looks better when it stands in relief against the quilting. Whatever background quilting I'm using, I almost always quilt an outline just outside the appliqués to emphasize that relief. That's not to say you can't quilt the appliqués—quilted details on appliqué shapes can be very effective when related to the appliqué to suggest movement, create texture, or define sections.

Straight, parallel lines with a walking foot are an easy quilting option, and they offer surprising variety: for the China Cupboard Wall Quilt (page 60), I let the quilting lines be imprecise to reflect the hand-drawn style of the appliqué; the striped fabric of the Cobblestones Quilt (page 48) made a built-in guide for straight lines; and for the Counterbalance Quilt (page 88), I bent the otherwise straight lines around the appliqués. Free-motion designs with a darning or free-motion foot can range from simple outlines to detailed patterns, and like appliqué, it just takes practice to make it feel like a natural process. I especially like to quilt a relatively dense meander in the appliqué backgrounds to make the appliqués themselves pop.

Time didn't allow the projects in the book to be handquilted, but handquilting and hand appliqué are obvious complements. Traditional handquilting produces a wonderful texture, while big-stitch quilting with pearl cotton has a fun, bold look and is quite a bit faster.

If you do decide to hire a long-arm quilter, try to see some samples of his or her work on other appliqué quilts. Many quilters do fabulous, intricate work that enhances appliqué, but others work exclusively in computerized, all-over patterns that charge

indiscriminately through any appliqué they encounter. My long-armer happens to be my mother, so I know she understands appliqué, as well as my taste and aesthetic. Long-arm quilting is a collaboration—my initial ideas for both Round the Block and Fruit Market were a little different, but what she did looks even better. The mechanics of long-arm setups allow different results than quilting on a domestic machine, so the long-armer should have a good idea of how best to take advantage of his/her machine and may well have some great suggestions. Some quilt shops can train you and rent time on a long-arm machine, so you can have the benefits of a long-arm and still do it yourself. Or perhaps you already own a long-arm machine—lucky you!

▲ *The combination of topstitched edges and a quilted outline give the motifs of the Pineapple Rings Lap Quilt (page 82) added dimension.*

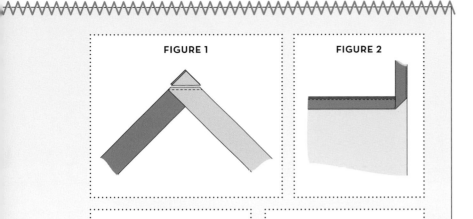

FIGURE 1   FIGURE 2

FIGURE 3   FIGURE 4

BINDING

Most of the projects in this book are bound with double-layer "French fold" binding. You can find lots of tips and tricks for this method on the Internet or in other books, but here's the basic process.

1 • Lay two binding strips (the number and width of the strips will be given in the project instructions) right sides together, at right angles. The area where the strips overlap forms a square. Sew diagonally across the square. Trim the excess fabric ¼" (6 mm) away from the seam line and press the seam allowances open **(fig. 1)**. Repeat to join all the strips, forming one long band.

2 • Fold the joined strip in half lengthwise with wrong sides together; press.

3 • Open the binding and press ½" (1.3 cm) to the wrong side at one short end. Refold the binding at the center crease. Starting with this folded-under end of the binding, place it near the center of bottom edge of the quilt, aligning the raw edges, and pin in place. Begin sewing the binding to the quilt, leaving several inches of the binding fabric free at the beginning. Stop sewing ¼" (6 mm) before reaching the corner, backstitch, and cut the threads.

4 • Rotate the quilt 90 degrees to position it for sewing the next side. To miter the corner, fold the binding fabric up, away from the project, at a 45-degree angle, then fold it back down along the quilt's raw edge **(figs. 2 and 3)**.

5 • Stitch the next side, beginning at the quilt's raw edge and ending ¼" (6 mm) from the next corner, as before. Continue sewing the remaining sides in the same way.

6 • Stop sewing a few inches from the beginning end of the binding fabric. Overlapping the pressed beginning end of the binding by at least ½" (1.3 cm), trim the working end to fit and tuck the raw working end inside the pressed beginning end of the binding. Finish sewing the binding to the quilt.

7 • Fold the binding over the raw edges of the quilt, enclosing them. The folded binding strip should just cover the stitches visible on the quilt back. Slip-stitch the binding to the backing fabric, tucking in the corners to complete the miters as you go **(fig. 4)**.

RAW-EDGE APPLIQUÉ

Fusible web takes the most intimidating part of appliqué—turning edges under—out of the equation, simplifying the process to little more than peel, stick, and stitch. Fraying is prevented by the fusible adhesive, and you can even trace the pattern shapes right onto the paper backing of the web. It couldn't be easier!

why raw-edge appliqué?

Some quilters consider appliqué that uses fusible web as "cheater's appliqué," but by definition, appliqué is simply a layer of fabric applied to the surface of another, and fusible web handles that application admirably. With my Mod Flowers Table Runner (page 44), for example, it keeps thick wool firmly in place on fluffy flannel, so it doesn't move while you're handstitching. Another objection sometimes made to fusible appliqué with regular quilting cotton is that it becomes too stiff, but this effect is greatly reduced with the methods I share in this chapter, which can even be adapted to improvisational projects such as the Cobblestones Quilt (page 48). Fused, machine-stitched optional; appliqué is durable, making it perfect for kids' quilts such as Round the Block (page 54). Aside from these practical advantages, the stitching used to hold down raw-edge shapes makes a visual outline around the appliqué, opening up opportunities to play with threads and stitches for decorative details, as I've done for the China Cupboard Wall Quilt (page 60).

Raw-Edge Appliqué at a Glance

TOOLBOX

- Paper-backed fusible web
- Iron
- Nonstick pressing sheet (optional)
- Craft knife and self-healing cutting mat
- Scissors
- Needles
- Thread
- Open-toe presser foot (for machine methods)
- Spray starch or stabilizer (optional; for machine methods)

PATTERNS AND TEMPLATES

- Use reversed pattern to trace shapes onto fusible web.
- Use non-reversed pattern to arrange shapes on single- or multi-layer background.
- Templates don't have seam allowances.

tools and supplies

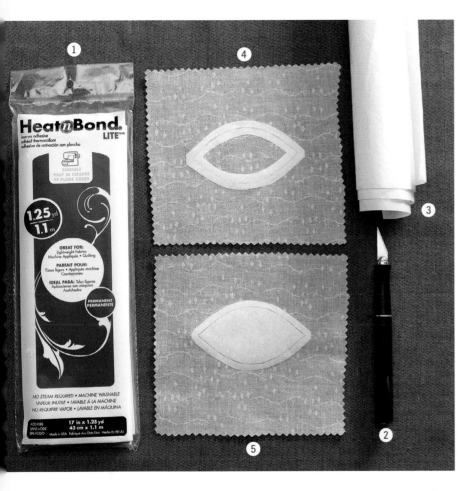

❶ Fusible web; ❷ Craft knife; ❸ Pressing sheet; ❹❺ Fusible web fused to wrong side of fabric, with and without center cut away.

Here's what you'll need to have on hand before you jump into raw-edge appliqué.

FUSIBLE WEB

Paper-backed fusible web can be pressed with an iron onto the wrong side of fabric, which can in turn be pressed onto another piece of fabric. With heavy-duty fusibles, that's it—no sewing required. For quilts, though, you'll generally want to use a lighter-weight fusible web designed to be sewn (these are made with adhesives that won't gum up your needle). One of the great things about fusible web is you can trace a pattern right onto the paper backing with a regular pencil, so it becomes a template as well as an adhesive. Many brands of fusible web are available, so use what works best for you. I like HeatnBond Lite because it doesn't require a damp press cloth, and the adhesive doesn't spontaneously separate from the paper as readily as some others do. Fusible webs are available as individual sheets, small rolls, or by the yard in various widths. The most common width is 17" (43 cm), so that's what the yardages in this chapter are based on.

Self-stick fusible web, such as Steam-A-Seam 2, includes a pressure-sensitive adhesive that can hold pieces in place temporarily before pressing to make the bond permanent. This is helpful for projects where you might want to try out appliqués in various locations, such as the cars in Round the Block, as well as for building complex appliqué designs piece by piece without committing straightaway to the final fuse.

PRESSING SHEET

A nonstick pressing sheet can protect your iron and ironing board from sticky fusible residue, but it's also great for assembling multi-piece fusible appliqués (page 35).

CUTTING TOOLS

To reduce stiffness by cutting away the interior fusible web from appliqué shapes, I find a craft knife, such as an X-Acto knife, used on a self-healing cutting mat far quicker than scissors.

Sewists have fabric scissors and paper scissors, and never the twain shall meet. But what about cutting through fused fabric with the paper backing still in place? I keep a third pair of scissors specifically for uses such as this. They're an older pair of fabric shears, retired from active fabric duty and now reserved for anything that might dull my new fabric scissors but needs a better blade than my plain paper scissors can offer.

OPEN-TOE PRESSER FOOT

For machine appliqué, an open-toe presser foot is extremely helpful for giving full visibility to the fabric edge, so you can see exactly where the needle is and where it needs to go as you keep sewing.

STABILIZERS

The fusible itself usually stabilizes the fabric somewhat to reduce the "tunneling" that can occur when the threads of an unstabilized zigzag stitch pull too tightly. A light spritz of spray starch on the background fabric, pressed dry, adds a little more firmness if

you're having trouble. For less well-behaved fabrics or when sewing with decorative stitches, back the background fabric with machine-embroidery stabilizer or improvise your own stabilizer. Tissue paper works well, as do the release papers of some fusible webs; just gently tear the paper away when the appliqué is finished.

NEEDLES AND THREAD

To sew the edges of fusible appliqué by machine, I usually use regular cotton sewing thread in a matching color. For stitching I want to be more prominent, such as satin and decorative stitches, the slightly heavier size 30 cotton embroidery thread gives a fuller cover with a bit of sheen. For real shine, try rayon machine-embroidery thread, but keep in mind that rayon doesn't have the abrasion resistance of cotton, so it may not be the best choice for quilts expected to get heavy wear.

I usually use machine-embroidery or sharp needles for sewing raw-edge appliqué. A size 75/11 needle, or close to it, works best for sewing with regular sewing thread on cotton fabric.

For sewing down fusible appliqués by hand, a blanket stitch with embroidery floss is common. I use this technique mostly for wool appliqué, for which I like to use a 50% wool, 50% acrylic thread that blends well with the felted fabrics. Whatever thread you're using, you'll want hand-embroidery needles (also called crewel needles) with an eye just large enough to accommodate the thread.

❶ Spools of cotton sewing thread and ❷ machine-embroidery needles are my supplies of choice for sewing raw-edge appliqué by machine.

For sewing raw-edge appliqué by hand, you can use ❸ embroidery floss; ❹ heavy cotton thread; ❺ wool thread (shown with a hand-embroidery needle); ❻ or pearl cotton.

techniques

Here are the basic processes you'll use for raw-edge fusible appliqué. Individual projects, whether in this book or other patterns you're using, may modify these general techniques for special purposes, so always read through the project instructions.

TRANSFERRING PATTERNS WITH FUSIBLE WEB

Follow these steps to trace templates or pattern pieces onto fusible web for easy transferring to your fabrics. For specialized techniques, though—such as the freehand approach used for the Cobblestones Quilt (page 48)—you'll use a modified form of this technique, as described in the project instructions. When working with fusible web, you'll be tracing shapes from a template or pattern that is a reverse of the final appliqué.

1 • Place fusible web paper side up over the pattern or template. (Use a light box or bright window if it's difficult to see the pattern lines, but fusible is usually thin enough to trace unaided.) Trace each shape needed onto the fusible web with a pencil **(fig. 1)**, leaving at least ½" (1.3 cm) between shapes. Label the fusible shapes if necessary to avoid confusion.

2 • Cut out the traced shapes, leaving a margin of about ¼" (6 mm) all around **(fig. 2)**.

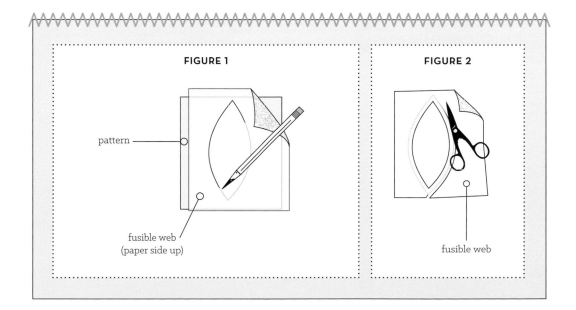

FIGURE 1

pattern

fusible web
(paper side up)

FIGURE 2

fusible web

3 • Place the traced shapes on a self-healing cutting mat and carefully cut out the inside of the shape using a craft knife, again leaving a margin of about ¼" (6 mm) **(fig. 3)**. (This optional step reduces the amount of fusible behind the shape to a small ring around the perimeter to reduce overall stiffness. I don't bother removing the insides from appliqués smaller than about ½" [1.3 cm] across or when fusing wool.)

4 • Press your appliqué fabric, if necessary, to remove wrinkles. Position the fusible shape paper side up on the wrong side of the fabric and fuse in place, following the fusible web manufacturer's instructions for iron temperature and other details **(fig. 4)**. Do not remove the release paper.

5 • When the fused fabric has cooled, cut the shape out along the traced line **(fig. 5)**.

6 • Peel the release paper off the appliqué piece and position the shape on the right side of the background fabric. (See Fusing Blocks on the next page for details on using a pattern to position multiple pieces.) Fuse the appliqué piece in place following manufacturer's instructions **(fig. 6)**.

❉ **tip**

Don't throw out the centers cut from your fusible shapes! They're still perfectly usable for smaller shapes. I have a whole box of fusible scraps, so I only have to cut into my roll of fusible web for big or oddly shaped pieces. Note though that fresh fusible does work best; the adhesive sometimes separates from the paper backing over time.

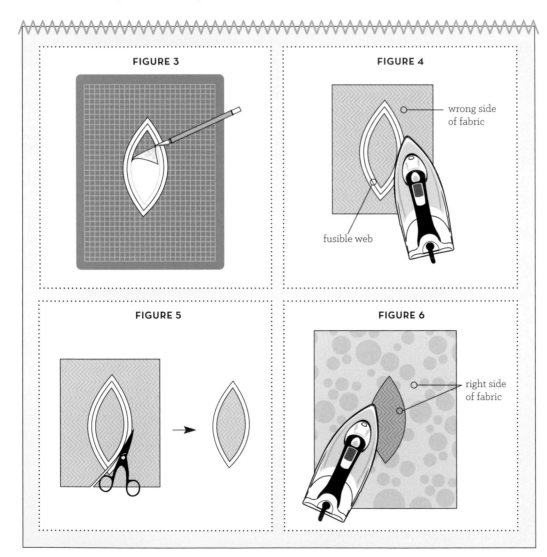

FIGURE 3

FIGURE 4

wrong side of fabric

fusible web

FIGURE 5

FIGURE 6

right side of fabric

FUSING LAYERED APPLIQUÉS

Where fused appliqués overlap each other, you'll want to make sure the lower piece has a sufficient extension under the top piece to prevent a gap between the two. Where pertinent in the patterns in this book, I've shown the overlap as a lighter line behind the piece on top, but for patterns that aren't as explicit, add a little less than ¼" (6 mm) to the overlapped edges of the visible shape when cutting the fused fabric. You may want to mark the paper backing of the fusible at these sections so you remember not to cut right on the line.

FUSING BLOCKS

For blocks with fusible appliqués layered on top of one another, I like to fuse the appliqués to each other before positioning them on the background. You'll need a right-way-round pattern, not the reversed pattern used for tracing templates. Follow Steps 1–5 of Transferring Patterns with Fusible Web (page 33) to prepare the individual appliqué pieces.

1 • Place the pattern right side up on your ironing surface. Cover it with a nonstick pressing sheet, which should be translucent enough to allow you to see the pattern lines (if not, thicken the pattern lines with a black marker) **(fig. 7)**.

2 • Leaving the release paper in place, position the lowermost appliqué piece (the instructions for each project will tell you which piece to start with) on the pressing sheet right side up, lining it up with its position on the pattern **(fig. 8)**.

3 • Peel off the release paper from a piece that will be layered directly on top, position it according to the pattern, and fuse it to the first piece **(fig. 9)**. Continue fusing pieces sequentially, working up to the uppermost layer of appliqué.

For multi-layer ▲ appliqués such as the cups block of the China Cupboard Wall Quilt (page 60), work from the bottom up.

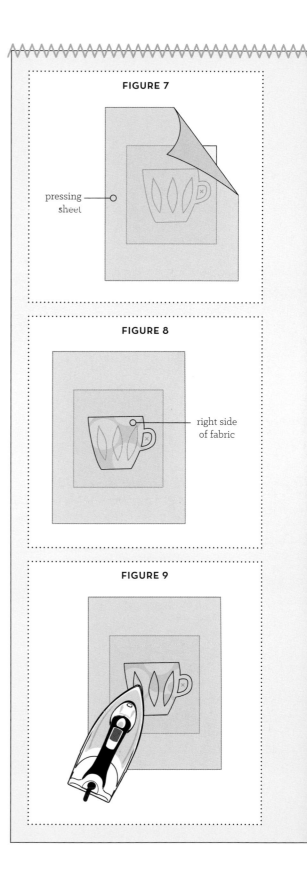

FIGURE 7

pressing sheet

FIGURE 8

right side of fabric

FIGURE 9

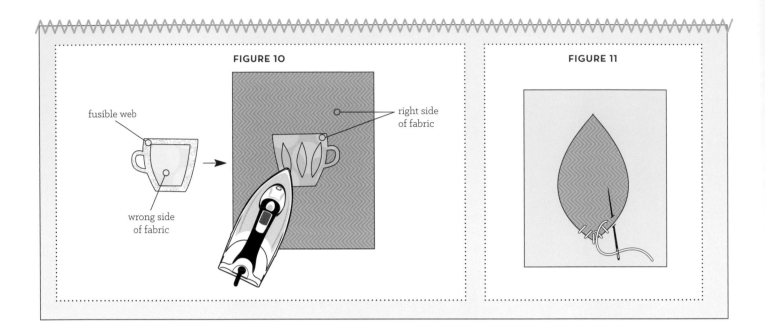

FIGURE 10

fusible web

wrong side
of fabric

right side
of fabric

FIGURE 11

4 · If any pieces extend outside the lower-most appliqué, they will temporarily stick to the pressing sheet; let the fused appliqué cool, then peel it away from the pressing sheet as a single unit.

5 · Remove the release paper from the lower-most appliqué piece and position it right side up on the background fabric according to the project instructions; fuse in place **(fig. 10)**.

SEWING BY HAND

I tend to reserve this technique for wool appliqué, but a blanket stitch can also be used when working with quilting cottons (I sometimes use it with broderie perse, see page 122). Matching or contrasting threads can be used, depending on whether you want to hide or show the stitches; try embroidery floss, pearl cotton, and wool-blend thread. In addition to the stitches described here, plenty of other decorative and utility stitches might be used to hold down the appliqué shapes—even a plain running stitch can look good.

Straight Overcast Stitch

Try to keep the distance between the stitches and the length of the individual stitches equal; the exact size will depend on the thread you choose and your intended effect.

1 · Knot the end of your thread. Bring the threaded needle up inside the appliqué shape.

2 · Take the thread down next to where it emerged, making the stitch perpendicular to the edge of the appliqué, just outside the edge.

3 · Bring the thread back up a stitch length away inside the appliqué shape **(fig. 11)**.

4 · Repeat Steps 2 and 3 all along the appliqué edge. Knot off the thread on the wrong side.

Blanket Stitch

Blanket stitch is very common for wool appliqué and other types of raw-edge appliqué. It creates a more prominent edge than an overcast stitch. Try it instead of the straight overcast stitch on the Mod Flowers Table Runner (page 44), or use it to handsew any of the fused projects in this

✿ *tip*

Unless I'm going for a contrasting edge, I match my thread color to the color of the fabric. (Err on the side of the thread being a shade darker than the fabric rather than lighter.) To minimize time spent rethreading your machine, sew all the pieces of a particular color at once (as far as the pieces' overlaps allow).

Mod Flowers Table ▶
Runner, page 44.

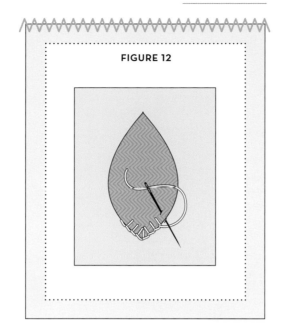

FIGURE 12

chapter. (Make smaller stitches on cotton fabrics than you would on wool and keep in mind that the stitching won't be as durable as machine sewing—I wouldn't recommend hand blanket stitches if you're planning to give Round the Block Kid's Quilt [page 54] to a child, for instance.)

1 • Knot the end of your thread. Bring the threaded needle up through the background fabric just next to the appliqué edge.

2 • Hold the thread away from the appliqué with the thumb of your non-sewing hand and insert the needle through the appliqué fabric a stitch length to the side and a stitch length from the appliqué's edge.

3 • Bring the needle back out of the background fabric just below the appliqué, making the stitch perpendicular to the edge of the appliqué, catching the held thread under the needle before pulling the thread through **(fig. 12)**.

4 • Repeat Steps 2 and 3 all along the appliqué edge. Knot off the thread on the wrong side when the shape's edges are all stitched.

If you need to start a new thread before the shape is finished, take the needle through the appliqué as normal, but do not bring it back through, leaving the tail on the wrong side and some slack in the loop remaining on the right side. Bring the next thread (knotted at the end) up through the loop, then pull the first thread's tail to tighten the loop. Fasten the loose tail of the first thread to the stitches on the wrong side and continue from Step 1 with the new thread.

SEWING BY MACHINE

Raw edges sewn by machine are more durable than those stitched by hand, as typically more of the raw edge is encased in stitches. For quilts that I expect to get a lot of wear, this is my go-to technique.

Zigzag Stitch

Available on all but the most basic sewing machines, a zigzag is the workhorse stitch of machine appliqué. Different threads, stitch lengths, and stitch widths can vary the appearance; here I describe the basic setup used for the projects in this chapter. Keeping the stitch open—that is, it's not a dense satin stitch—avoids a heavy buildup

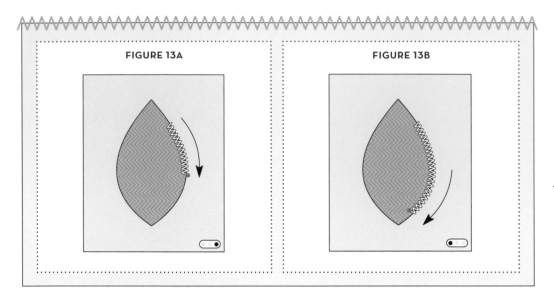

FIGURE 13A

FIGURE 13B

◄ On the right swing (fig. 13a), the needle falls just outside the appliqué; on the left swing (fig. 13b), the needle falls inside the appliqué.

of thread along the edges of the appliqué and works somewhat like an accordion to bend around edges.

1 • Thread the sewing machine with size 50 sewing thread (use the same thread in the bobbin). Install an open-toe presser foot, if available.

2 • Set the machine for a zigzag stitch 1 to 2 mm wide, with a stitch length of 1 mm or slightly less (i.e., 1 mm between the stitches). Always sew a sample on scraps of similar fabrics to determine if tension adjustments need to be made: no bobbin thread should show on the right side. If available, engage the machine's needle-down function for easy turning of corners and guiding curves.

3 • Place the work right side up under the presser foot and lower the needle partway. Position the work so the needle will enter the background fabric just to the side of the appliqué (the needle should be on the outer swing when starting). Lower the presser foot, hold both top and bobbin threads, and take a stitch or two. The outer swing of the needle should continue to just graze the appliqué fabric but not catch it **(fig. 13a)**, while

the inner swing catches both layers **(fig. 13b)**. Let go of the threads and continue sewing with the needle's outer swing following the outside edge of the appliqué.

4 • Sew all the way around the appliqué to the starting point (if the shape is uninterrupted by another layer of appliqué); the zigzag should meet the start of the stitching, but stop just short of overlapping it. Cut the threads, leaving a tail of several inches. Take all thread ends on the top of the appliqué to the wrong side, either by threading them into a hand needle or carefully pulling them out of the last stitches on the wrong side. Knot all four threads (two top and two bobbin threads) together and/or thread them on a hand needle and slide them under about ½" (1.3 cm) of zigzag stitching on the wrong side, then clip the excess thread tails.

DEALING WITH OUTSIDE CURVES
Gentle curves can often be sewn just by guiding the fabric by hand as you sew, but you'll need to pause and turn the fabric when dealing with smaller appliqués.

Stop with the needle down in the fabric on its outer swing, lift the presser foot, and

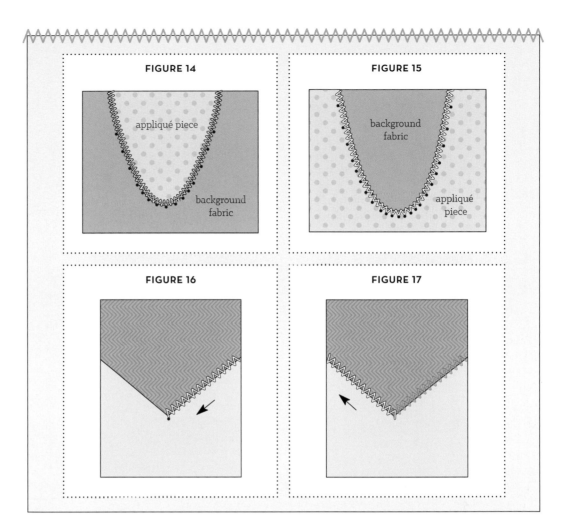

FIGURE 14

appliqué piece

background fabric

FIGURE 15

background fabric

appliqué piece

FIGURE 16

FIGURE 17

Red dots indicate ▶ pivot points.

pivot the work so the next stitch will remain perpendicular to the appliqué fabric edge. Sew more stitches as normal, then pivot on another outer swing. The number of stitches between pivots will depend on the depth of the curve: tighter turns will need more frequent pivots **(fig. 14)**.

DEALING WITH INSIDE CURVES

Concave curves are dealt with in the opposite way to their convex cousins.

1 • Stop with the needle down in the fabric on its inner swing, lift the presser foot, and pivot the work so the next stitch will remain perpendicular to the appliqué fabric edge.

2 • Sew more stitches as normal, then pivot on another inner swing. Tighter turns will need more frequent pivots **(fig. 15)**.

DEALING WITH OUTSIDE POINTS

For many points, you can just stitch along one side up to the point, stopping to pivot with the needle in the background right at the tip of the point **(fig. 16)**, then sew along the next side, overlapping the last few stitches of the first side **(fig. 17)**. Pieces that taper to a sharper point than your stitch is wide are a little trickier: progressively slant your stitches away from perpendicular to the edge as you approach the point **(fig. 18)**, then slant them back out to perpendicular as

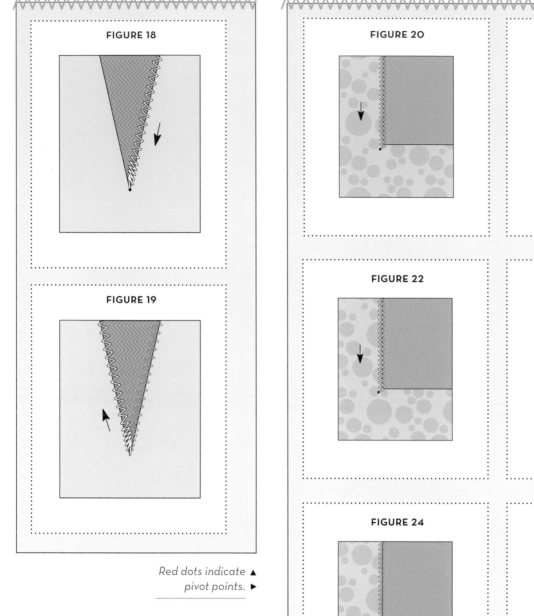

FIGURE 18

FIGURE 19

Red dots indicate ▲
pivot points. ▶

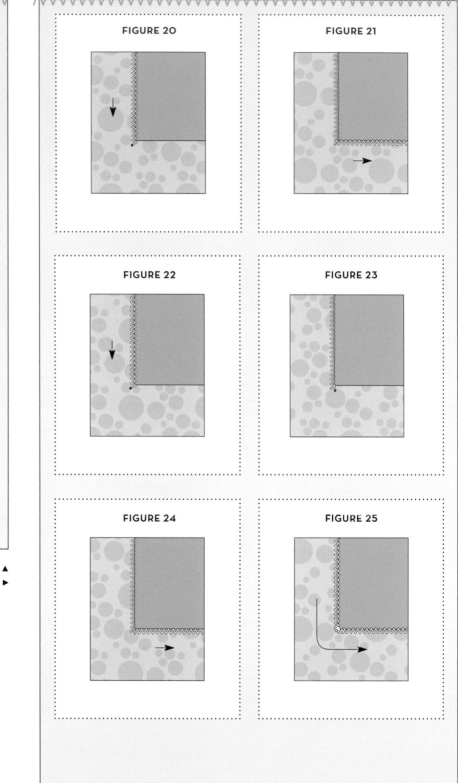

FIGURE 20

FIGURE 21

FIGURE 22

FIGURE 23

FIGURE 24

FIGURE 25

you come out of the point on the other side **(fig. 19)**. If your sewing machine allows you to smoothly taper the stitch width, narrow the zigzag somewhat as you approach the point, too.

DEALING WITH INSIDE CORNERS

For square corners, keep sewing a zigzag beyond the corner for slightly less than the

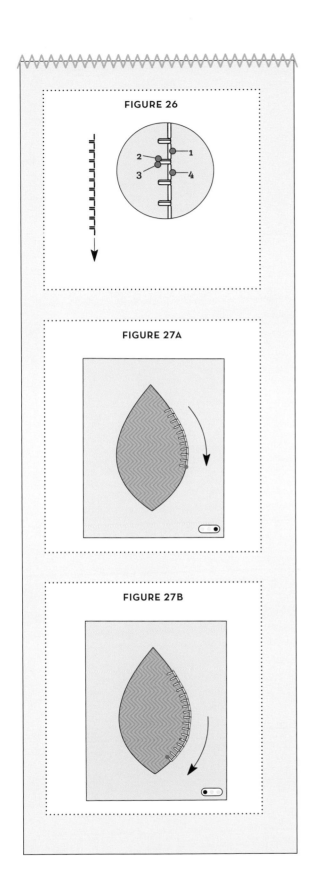

FIGURE 26

FIGURE 27A

FIGURE 27B

*Zigzag stitching ▲
is a functional
choice for kids'
quilts such as
Round the Block
(page 54).*

◄ *On the right swing,
the needle falls just
to the side of the
appliqué, making
straight stitches
(fig. 27a); on the left
swing of the needle,
straight stitches
are made into the
appliqué (fig. 27b).*

width of your stitch (for example, a 2 mm wide stitch should keep going not quite 2 mm past the corner). Stop and pivot on the inside swing of the needle **(fig. 20)**, then sew the next side of the corner **(fig. 21)**. To keep the stitching smooth on the first side of the corner, I usually pivot only about half of the angle of the corner, then pivot to perpendicular with the edge on the next stitch **(figs. 22–24)**. To round a corner, slant the inside of the stitches toward the corner as you are entering and sewing away from it **(fig. 25)**.

Blanket Stitch

Many computerized sewing machines are equipped with one or more blanket stitches. The best machine blanket stitch for appliqué sews one straight stitch (labeled 1 in **fig. 26**), a stitch directly to the left (2) and another back (3), and then the next straight stitch (4). This can be used much as the zigzag stitch described above, with the straight stitches following the outer edge of the appliqué on the background fabric and the perpendicular stitches "biting" into the appliqué shape **(figs. 27a and 27b)**.

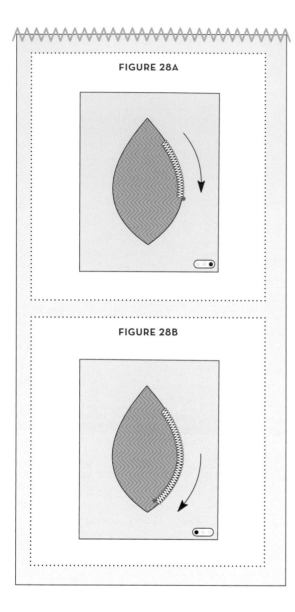

FIGURE 28A

FIGURE 28B

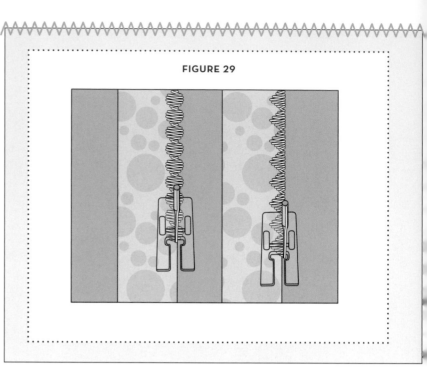

FIGURE 29

Satin Stitch

A machine satin stitch **(figs. 28a and 28b)** is simply a dense zigzag that appears as a smooth bead of thread; it's perfect for when you want a strong contrast-color line to define the edges of your appliqués. Satin stitching can be finicky: stitch too far apart and it's just a zigzag, but stitch too close together and the thread piles up and the machine can't advance the fabric. Experiment with tension, stitch length and width, and

threads to find out what works best with your machine and look for a presser foot with a channel on the bottom to give the built-up stitches room (most open-toe feet have such a channel).

Decorative Stitches

Any of your machine's stitches could potentially form a decorative edge around your appliqués. It's easiest to limit yourself to stitches that move in only one direction; "stretch" stitches move the fabric backward and forward while sewing, which makes it more difficult to guide. My favorites are decorative satin stitches: balls, scallops, triangles, and other simple shapes repeated along the stitching line. If your machine, like mine, doesn't allow you to alter the density of such stitches (that is, if it sews a complete ball shape in ten stitches whether you set the stitch length to 0.5 mm or 5 mm), use a heavier or finer thread to keep the shapes filled in appropriately. I used size 30 machine-embroidery and size 40 machine-quilting

▲ *Scalloped satin stitches add decorative detail to the jug block in the China Cupboard Wall Quilt (page 60).*

cotton threads to keep the decorative stitches in the China Cupboard Wall Quilt (page 60) filled in smoothly.

An open-toe foot is crucial for decorative satin stitches, and you'll want to sew a sample on fused fabric to determine where the stitch should be placed in relation to the appliqué edges. The stitching should completely cover the edge, so the outer swing of the needle should be in the background fabric just to the side of the appliqué at the narrowest point of the stitched pattern. This point won't always be at the center needle position, where you might expect it **(fig. 29)**.

Decorative and satin stitches can also be used without appliqué to add detail lines to appliqué blocks, like the lines of ball-pattern stitching on the pot block in my China Cupboard Wall Quilt. Narrow stems could be made this way—a triangular stitch could look like the thorny stem of a rose.

Topstitched Edges

Straight stitching close to the appliqué edges is probably the quickest and easiest way to sew down fused shapes. Of course, it leaves a true raw edge on the finished piece. Though the fusible usually prevents too much fraying, I tend to employ this technique when I want the edges to fray slightly as a design element. (I didn't use topstitching with any of the raw-edge projects in this book, but for a topstitch technique with a turned edge, see page 81.)

MOD FLOWERS TABLE RUNNER

APPLIQUÉ TECHNIQUE
Raw-edge wool appliqué

FINISHED SIZE
14½ " × 42" (37 × 106.5 cm)

MATERIALS
- ○ ½ yd (45.5 cm) printed cotton flannel for background
- ○ Assorted scraps of felted wool for flower, leaf, and stem appliqués (see Step 4)
- ○ ½ yd (45.5 cm) quilting cotton or flannel backing fabric
- ○ ¼ yd (23 cm) flannel binding fabric
- ○ 22" × 50" (56 × 127 cm) batting
- ○ ⅝ yd (57 cm) paper-backed fusible web
- ○ Wool thread or embroidery floss to coordinate with felted wool

TOOLS
- ○ Appliqué pattern (pattern insert B)
- ○ Toolbox for raw-edge appliqué (page 30)

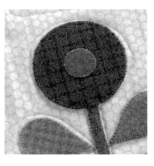

There's no better place to start with appliqué than felted wool. It doesn't fray when cut, and the fluffy fabric is invitingly touchable. The dimensional quality of the thick wool makes it literally stand out even in the simple geometric shapes used here, and the softness of the felt plays off the very defined edges of those shapes.

Not all the wools I used had been felted to the same extent, so using fusible web ensures they're true to the fray-free promise (without having to refelt everything and subsequently clean masses of loose wool out of your washing machine).

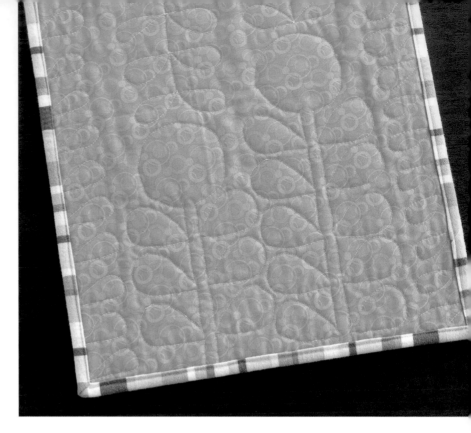

PREPARE THE BACKGROUND FABRIC

Flannel can shrink significantly, so pre-washing is strongly recommended.

1 • From the flannel, cut 1 strip 15" (38 cm) wide × width of fabric. To keep the fabric straight, cut into the selvedge and tear the fabric instead of cutting across it (the torn edges will be trimmed away later, so don't worry about the distortion along the edges).

2 • Zigzag along the torn edges to prevent them from fraying when you work the appliqué.

3 • Lightly press the background piece in half lengthwise to mark the center.

PREPARE THE APPLIQUÉS

4 • Trace 32 Leaf, 2 Stem A, 2 Stem B, 4 Flower, and 4 Flower Center shapes onto the paper side of the fusible web. Fuse to the wrong side of the corresponding felted wool. (I used 4 green felts, alternating 2 for the leaves of each flower; this required cutting 8 Leaves from each green felt.) You may need to experiment with iron settings to fuse the web fully; I find that steam helps my fusible web adhere to wool. Cut out each shape on the traced lines.

5 • Transfer the appliqué pattern onto each end of the background piece, aligning the center dashes of the pattern with the center crease on the background and placing the dashed bottom line of the pattern about ¼" (6 mm) in from the selvedges. You may be able to use a light box to trace the pattern if your flannel is a light color or try another transfer method (page 22).

APPLIQUÉ THE SHAPES

6 • Position the Stem pieces on the background and fuse in place. Then position and fuse the Leaf and Flower pieces. For added interest, alternate the green wool Leaf colors within each flower.

7 • Handsew around each felted wool piece with a straight overcast stitch (page 37) using coordinating thread.

QUILT AND FINISH

After quilting around the appliqué shapes, I filled the space between the two "blocks" with vines of leaves based on the appliquéd leaf shapes.

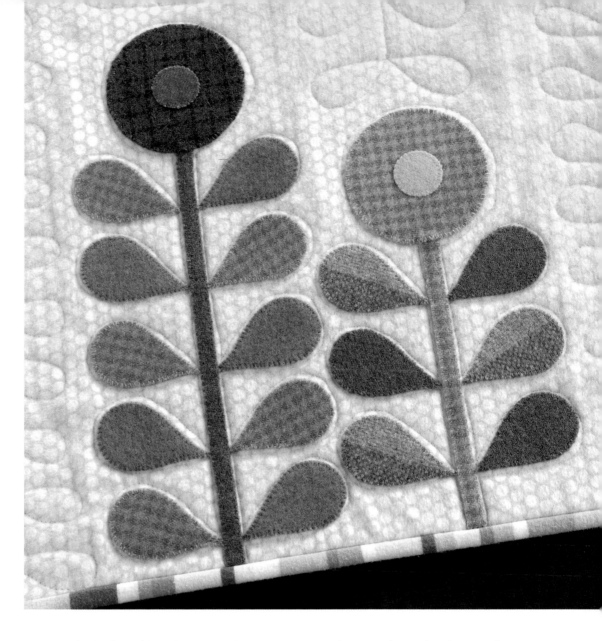

variations

Blanket stitch is probably the most popular finish for wool appliqué and defines the edge more than the overcasting I've used. Other hand-embroidery stitches are options, too, even the humble running stitch.

I kept the emphasis on the simple shapes for my runner, but wool felt seems to naturally encourage embellishment—try using the pattern as a starting point for adding decorative stitches and fibers, buttons, or whatever else strikes your eye.

8 • Baste the backing fabric, batting, and runner top together. Quilt as desired. Trim the excess batting, backing, and top, squaring the runner edges while trimming the selvedges and zigzagged edges of the background flannel. Make sure the appliquéd flowers are centered between the long edges of the runner, which should now be 14" to 14½" (35.5 to 37 cm) wide, and check that the stem ends are no more than ¼" (6 mm) from the short runner ends.

9 • Cut three 2¼" (5.5 cm) wide strips from the binding flannel (the extra width of these strips accommodates the thickness of the flannel when folded), join them with diagonal seams, and press in half wrong sides together. Bind the runner.

COBBLESTONES QUILT

APPLIQUÉ TECHNIQUE
Improvisational fused
raw-edge appliqué

FINISHED SIZE
80" × 100" (203 × 254 cm); to fit a
queen-size bed

MATERIALS
○ 6½ yd (6 m) lengthwise stripe
  fabric for background

○ 2½ yd (2.3 m) total assorted solid
  and print fabrics for appliqués,
  each piece at least 8½" × 8½"
  (21.5 × 21.5 cm)

○ 7 yd (6.4 m) backing fabric

○ ⅔ yd (61 cm) binding fabric

○ 88" × 108" (223.5 × 274.3 cm)
  batting

○ 4½ yd (4.2 m) paper-backed
  fusible web

TOOLS
○ Toolbox for raw-edge appliqué
  (page 30)

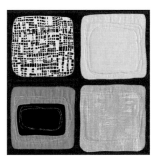

Fusible appliqué is often a connect-the-dots process: most instructions (including those in this book) assume you're working from a pattern you want to reproduce faithfully. For this quilt, I've adapted the method to suit a more improvisational approach that still keeps the center of the appliqués free of stiffness-causing fusible. The concentrated "path" of the cobblestone blocks across the center of the quilt gives the simple shapes more impact, and the path is placed so that impact is optimized when the quilt is on a bed. As a practical bonus, a swath of appliqué blocks between two large pieces of plain fabric greatly simplifies construction!

choosing fabric

We tend to think of modern design as clean and spare, but my inspiration for this quilt's fabrics was the less-minimalistic graphic design of the early 1950s, when solid areas of color often found themselves alongside blotchy painted textures and sketch-like markings. The colors and shapes of this quilt are inspired by a fabric design by textile artist Jacqueline Groag.

CUT THE FABRIC

1 • From striped background fabric, cut lengthwise:

> ▷ 1 Upper rectangle 40½" × 80½" (103 × 204.5 cm)
>
> ▷ 1 Lower rectangle 28½" × 80½" (72.5 × 204.5 cm)
>
> ▷ 40 Background squares, 8½" × 8½" (21.5 × 21.5 cm).

2 • From fusible web, cut: 40 squares 8" × 8" (20.5 × 20.5 cm).

APPLIQUÉ

3 • Cutting freehand with a craft knife, remove about a 6½" (16.5 cm) square from the center of each 8" (20.5 cm) fusible web square **(fig. 1)**. Retain the cut-away web for use in Step 8.

4 • Press the 8" (20.5 cm) fusible web squares onto the wrong side of the assorted appliqué fabrics. Roughly cut out a 7¼" to 7½" (18.5 to 19 cm) square with scissors, rounding the corners slightly. The sides don't need to be perfectly straight: follow the general contours of the shape originally removed from the fusible web, making sure to retain a perimeter web margin of about ¼" (6 mm) **(fig. 2)**. If it helps, draw a line to follow on the paper side of the fusible web before cutting it out; I found just spontaneously cutting to be easier and quicker. Cut a total of 40 rounded squares.

5 • Center a rounded-off fabric square fusible side down on each Background square's right side and fuse in place.

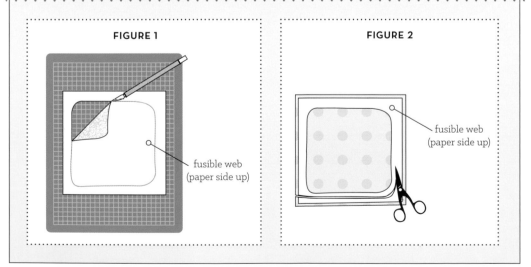

FIGURE 1

fusible web (paper side up)

FIGURE 2

fusible web (paper side up)

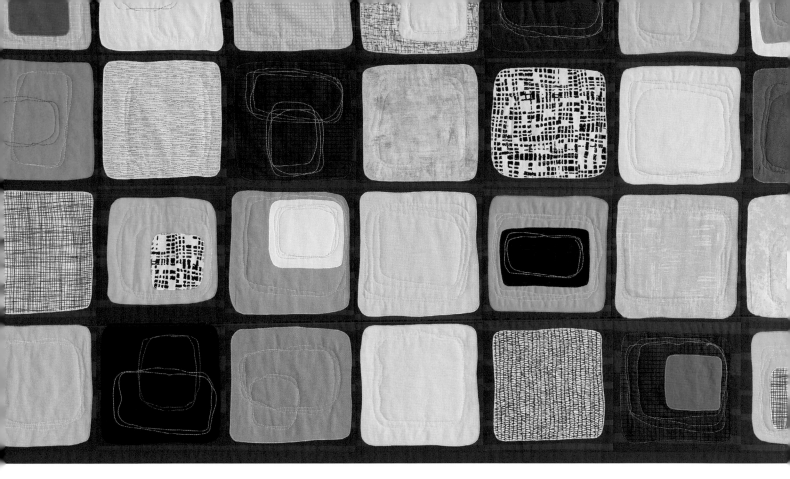

Improvisational Raw-Edge Appliqué

Freeform fusible appliqué is nothing new; many art quilters simply add fusible to large pieces of fabric and cut shapes as the spirit moves them. Some of these quilters recommend special extra-thin fusible web to minimize stiffness. Many of them leave the edges completely raw, counting on heavy quilting to reinforce the fusible.

For functional and decorative quilts, rather than works of art, I instead wanted to adapt my usual stitched raw-edge method and supplies to freer shapes without sacrificing the cutaway inside fusible. It occurred to me that the craft knife I already use to cut away the inside shapes was perfect for cutting freehand. All I had to do was cut the inside away first, and then the fused fabric could be cut roughly following the edge cut by the craft knife. As long as the squares of fusible I was starting from were the same each time, I could be sure whatever appliqués I cut from them would fit on the backgrounds.

Note that the instructions give plenty of dimensions to guide the cutting of these "freehand" shapes—improvisation to me is more about embracing imprecision within a planned framework than complete freewheeling. I usually know the general idea of how I want a quilt to look, and then I come up with a way to make it using one of my standard bag-of-tricks methods or a new one. So I often end up improvising the process itself even more than the individual design elements. I hope this book will spark your own experimentation in form and process!

6 • Sew around each fused square with a zig-zag stitch (page 37) using matching thread. Pivot every couple stitches at the corners to keep them smooth.

7 • Arrange the appliquéd blocks in 4 rows of 10 blocks each on a design wall or other flat work surface, distributing the colors and values of the fabrics until you're satisfied with the layout. I kept the striped backgrounds running the same direction, but you could also try alternating them for a basketweave design.

8 • Consider which of your sewn blocks would benefit from the addition of another square or rectangle. The sample quilt has eleven of these smaller shapes, generally different in value from the square fabric behind them, and I avoided putting two busy prints together. The smallest of these shapes in the sample is about 3½" (9 cm) square. Using the fusible web cut away in Step 3, cut as many smaller squares and rectangles with their centers removed as you'd like. Since you're using scraps of fusible cut from the main squares, the maximum size is already limited. Fuse these web shapes onto the wrong side of the remaining appliqué fabric, then cut out the shape as for the larger squares in Step 4. Fuse the secondary shapes to the main squares of the appliquéd blocks, referring to the project photo for positioning suggestions or placing them as desired. Sew around each secondary shape with a zigzag stitch in matching thread.

9 • Return the blocks to the design wall or flat work surface and rearrange to distribute the secondary shapes or make any other final layout alterations.

ASSEMBLE THE QUILT TOP

10 • Sew the rows of blocks together. Press the seam allowances to one side, alternating the direction for adjacent rows.

11 • Pin and sew adjacent rows together in sets of two, aligning the seams, then pin and sew the two sets together. Press the seam allowances to one side.

12 • Pin and sew the Upper rectangle to one of the long raw edges of the pieced block section. Pin and sew the Lower rectangle to the remaining long edge. Press the seam allowances to one side.

QUILT AND FINISH

I quilted this project on my domestic sewing machine, mainly to prove large quilts don't require a long-armer! The large size means a lot of bulk to force through the machine throat, so for the majority of the quilt, I stuck to straight lines, letting the feed dogs and walking foot do the work. By following the fabric stripe, I avoided all marking and still kept the lines straight (the stripes in the fabric are actually a little irregular—all the better!). For the squares themselves, I free-motion quilted overlapping, rounded-off squarish shapes to emphasize the shapes of the appliqué. If you're daunted by quilting something so big, this could be fairly economical to hire a long-armer to quilt, with an allover pattern in the Upper and Lower sections.

13 • Cut the backing into two 3½ yd (3.2 m) sections. Sew these sections together with a vertical seam to make a backing of at least 88" × 108" (223.5 × 274.3 cm).

14 • Baste the backing, batting, and quilt top together. Quilt as desired. Trim the excess batting and backing and square the edges of the quilt.

15 • From binding fabric, cut 10 strips 2" (5 cm) × width of fabric. Join the binding strips with diagonal seams and press in half wrong sides together. Bind the quilt.

ROUND THE BLOCK KID'S QUILT

APPLIQUÉ TECHNIQUE
Fused raw-edge appliqué

FINISHED SIZE
41" × 49" (104 × 124.5 cm)

MATERIALS
○ 1¼ yd (114.5 cm) dark gray print for road borders

○ 1¼ yd (114.5 cm) gray-and-white crosswise stripe for lane-marking border; ¼ yd (23 cm) for a length-wise stripe

○ ¾ yd (68.5 cm) total assorted cityscape prints for center (trees, shops, parks, traffic, etc.); if using scraps, each should be at least 9" × 9" (23 × 23 cm)

○ 10 pieces assorted bright solid fabrics for vehicle appliqués, at least the following sizes:

  ○ 2 for Buses 12" × 5" (30.5 × 12.5 cm)

  ○ 1 for Truck 9" × 5" (23 × 12.5 cm)

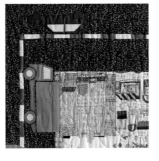

Just as there are all sorts of cars on the road, built by companies all over the world, the cars in this quilt come from road signs of various countries—the hatchback and bus are German, the sedan American, and the truck Italian. The pictographic silhouettes make for simple, bold appliqués circling a center pieced from assorted townscape prints to suggest a city block. Using self-stick fusible web allows you to move the vehicles around before committing to a final composition; placing the vehicles over the seam lines engages them with their environment. With securely stitched appliqué edges, the quilt is ready for its own natural environment—a child's playroom.

Continued on next page...▼

. . . continued from previous page.

○ 3 for Sedans 9½" × 4"
  (24 × 10 cm)

○ 4 for Hatchbacks 8" × 3½"
  (20.5 × 9 cm)

○ ⅛ yd (11.5 cm) white solid fabric
  for detail appliqués

○ 1½ yd (1.4 m) backing fabric

○ ⅓ yd (30.5 cm) binding fabric

○ 49" × 57" batting (124.5 × 145 cm)

○ ⅞ yd (80 cm) paper-backed
  fusible web (self-stick
  recommended)

○ Tear-away stabilizer (optional)

TOOLS

○ Digital camera

○ Vehicle patterns (pattern insert B)

○ Toolbox for raw-edge appliqué
  (page 30)

choosing fabric

In a visual sense, contrast usually refers to the juxtaposition of light and dark, but more broadly, any two opposed things make a contrast. I like to play with the contrast between solid and printed fabrics in my quilts, for example. Solids are well suited to the iconic road-sign vehicles, and they stand on their own all the better for being placed on a "road" of printed tonal fabric. Using more pictorial townscape prints in the center of the quilt gives the design another layer of depth.

CUT THE FABRIC

1 • From assorted cityscape prints, cut:

▷ 12 squares 8½" × 8½" (21.5 × 21.5 cm).

2 • From dark gray print, cut:

▷ 4 Inner Borders 4½" × 32½"
  (11.5 × 82.5 cm)

▷ 4 Outer Borders 4½" × 41½"
  (11.5 × 105.5 cm).

3 • From gray-and-white stripe, cut:

▷ 2 Short Stripe Borders 1" × 33½"
  (2.5 × 85 cm)

▷ 2 Long Stripe Borders 1" × 40½"
  (2.5 × 103 cm).

ASSEMBLE THE QUILT

To allow the appliquéd vehicles to extend over seam lines, the entire quilt top needs to be pieced before appliquéing.

4 • Referring to the Assembly Diagram (page 59), arrange the cityscape squares in 4 rows of 3 blocks each, orienting any directional prints to face outward all around the center section. (For the sample, I used 2 squares of tree prints instead of city buildings in the very center, as if there were a park or courtyard surrounded by the buildings of the outer squares.)

5 • Piece the rows of cityscape squares together. Press the seam allowances to one side, alternating the direction for each row.

6 • Pin 2 sets of adjacent rows together, aligning the seam allowances, then pin and sew the 2 halves together forming the Center.

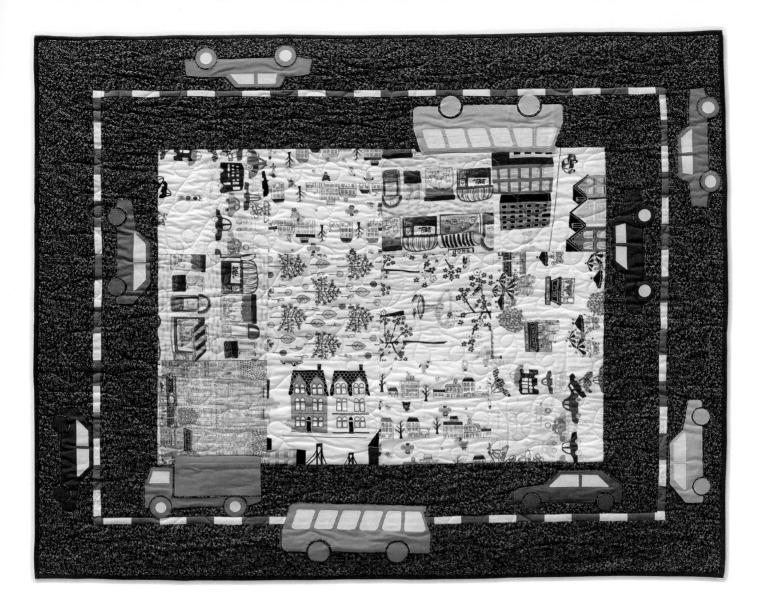

7 • Pin and sew an Inner Border along each long edge of the pieced Center. Press the seam allowances toward the borders. Pin and sew the remaining Inner Borders to the top and bottom edges of the Center section. Press the seam allowances toward the borders.

8 • Pin and sew a Long Stripe Border along each long edge of the quilt top. Press the seam allowances toward the stripe. Pin and sew the Short Stripe Borders to the top and bottom edges of the quilt top. Press the seam allowances toward the stripe.

9 • Pin and sew an Outer Border along each long edge of the quilt top. Press the seam allowances toward the Outer Borders. Pin and sew the remaining Outer Borders to the top and bottom edges of the quilt top, then press the seam allowances toward the Outer Borders.

PREPARE THE APPLIQUÉS
10 • Trace the vehicle and wheel shapes onto fusible web as directed on the patterns (or as desired, if you want to alter the number, type, or direction of the vehicles). Cut out the centers, leaving at least ¼" (6 cm) around

the perimeter. Fuse to the wrong side of the chosen fabric for each vehicle, then cut the shapes on the drawn lines. Trace the vehicle details (windows and hubcaps) onto fusible web, then fuse the web to the white fabric wrong side and cut out.

11 • Position the vehicle detail pieces on the corresponding vehicles and fuse them in place. Do not remove the release paper from the vehicle bodies or wheels yet.

APPLIQUÉ THE VEHICLES

12 • Sew around each detail piece with a zig-zag stitch (see page 37) using white thread; you may want to use a stabilizer behind the stitching to prevent puckering. To keep the curve smooth around the small hub-cap circles, pivot about every fourth stitch. Remove the stabilizer.

13 • With the assembled quilt top on a design wall or other flat work surface, arrange the vehicles as shown in the photo or as desired. I kept clockwise-traveling vehicles to the inner lane and counterclockwise ones to the outer lane, but I let the tops of the vehicles cross over the seam lines with the stripe and cityscape prints to add a sense of perspective. I placed the wheels and the truck's trailer by eye; refer to the patterns if you need more guidance. Take a digital photo of the quilt top to refer to as you continue.

14 • Fuse all pieces of one of the vehicles to the quilt top. (You could fuse all the vehicles in place before proceeding, but I found it easier to work with a single vehicle at a time so I didn't have to worry about other fused pieces coming loose while appli-quéing.) Zigzag around the edges of the vehicle pieces.

15 • Refer to the photo you took in Step 13 to reposition the next vehicle. Fuse and sew as described in Step 14. Continue until all vehicles are sewn down.

QUILT AND FINISH

The sample was quilted on a long-arm machine, but the design could be easily free-motion quilted on a domestic machine. The background is lightly filled with sprawling loops to suggest motion, and each vehicle is outlined to define it against the background.

16 • Baste the backing, batting, and quilt top together. Quilt as desired. Trim the excess batting and backing, and square the edges of the quilt when finished.

17 • From binding fabric, cut 5 strips 2" (5 cm) × width of fabric. Join the binding strips with diagonal seams and press in half wrong sides together. Bind the quilt.

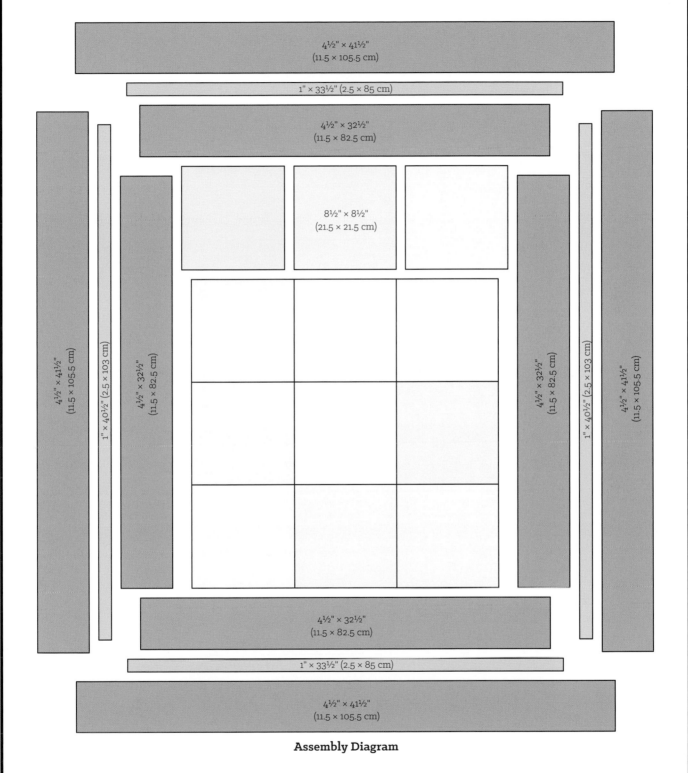

Assembly Diagram

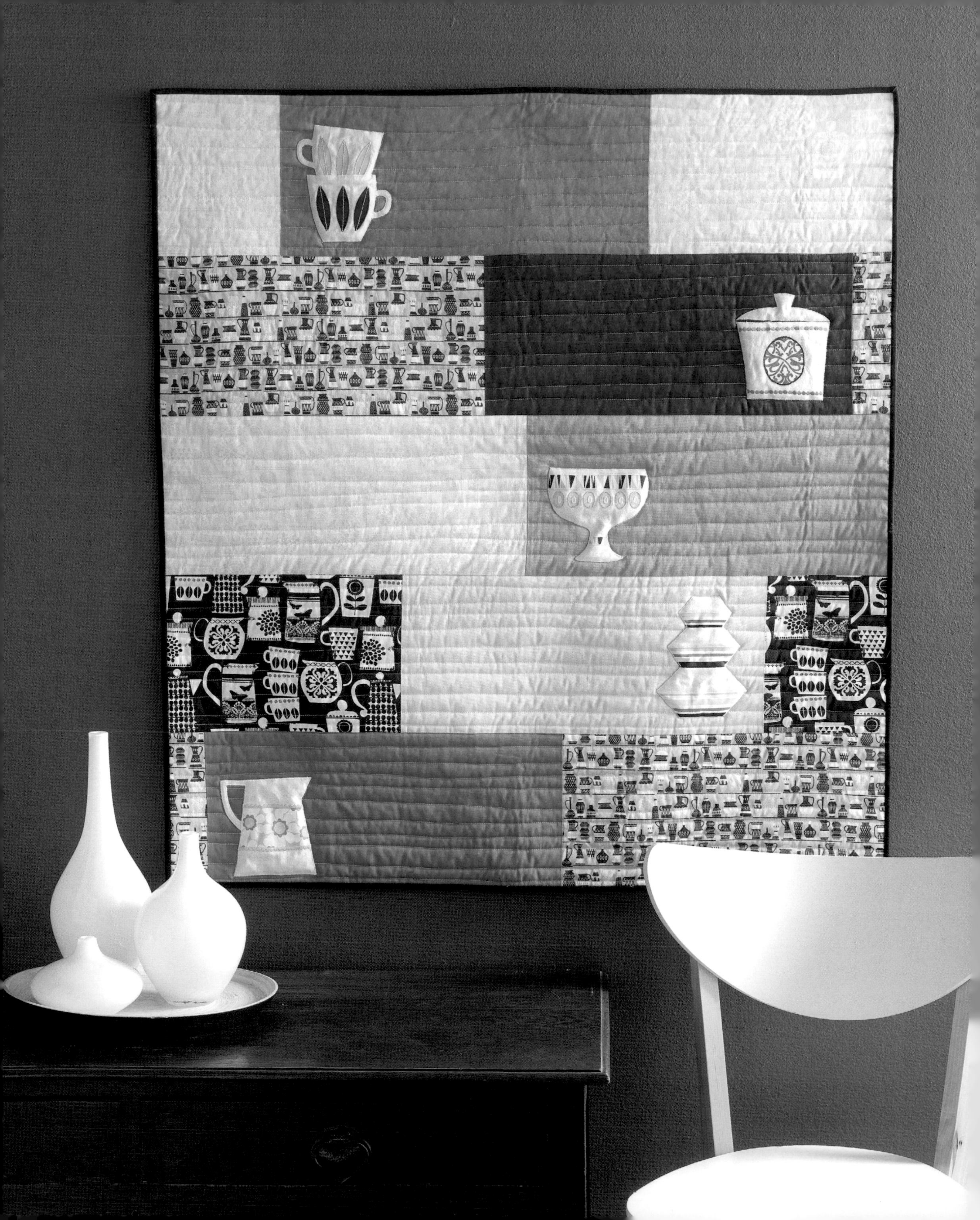

CHINA CUPBOARD WALL QUILT

TECHNIQUE
Fused raw-edge appliqué with decorative stitches

FINISHED SIZE
36" × 40" (91.5 × 101.5 cm)

MATERIALS
○ ⅜ yd (34.5 cm) each of 5 blue solid fabrics for backgrounds

○ ⅜ yd (34.5 cm) each of 3 to 5 assorted pottery prints (sample shows 3 fabrics, but a different one could be used for each row if desired)

○ ¼ yd (23 cm) white solid fabric for appliqués

○ Assorted scraps of coordinating solids and prints for appliqué details

○ 1⅓ yd (1.2 m) backing fabric

○ ¼ yd (23 cm) binding fabric

○ 44" × 48" (112 × 122 cm) batting

○ ⅓ yd (30.5 cm) paper-backed fusible web

○ Coordinating decorative threads

Continued on next page . . . ▼

As a kid, one of my favorites of my mom's quilts was one that looked like shelves full of teacups, many of which were fabric re-creations of actual teacups from her mother and grandmother. Nowadays my mom and I both quilt, and we both compulsively collect more dishes than we can possibly use. I designed China Cupboard as a nod to her teacup quilt but made with an aesthetic closer to the dishes I prefer. Though my quilt doesn't replicate real dishes, it nevertheless reminds me of the interests I share with my mother and previous generations of our family.

. . . *continued from previous page.*

TOOLS

○ China Cupboard patterns (pattern insert B)

○ Light box

○ Toolbox for raw-edge appliqué (page 30)

choosing fabric

In some ways, I collect dishes and fabric similarly: I fixate on a particular color combination or style and want to collect lots of different pieces that have that common element. Here, the prints' shades of blue (ranging from aqua to navy) define the quilt's color scheme, and the hand-drawn style of the prints further unifies them and sets the tone for the appliqués.

CUT THE FABRIC

1 • From each shade of blue solid fabric cut:

▷ 1 rectangle 8½" × 18½" (21.5 × 47 cm).

2 • From pottery prints, using the same fabric for each row, cut:

▷ Row 1: 1 rectangle 8½" × 6½" (21.5 × 16.5 cm) and 1 rectangle 8½" × 12½" (21.5 × 31.5 cm)

▷ Row 2: 1 rectangle 8½" × 16½" (21.5 × 42 cm) and 1 rectangle 8½" × 2½" (21.5 × 6.5 cm)

▷ Row 3: 1 rectangle 8½" × 18½" (21.5 × 47 cm)

▷ Row 4: 1 rectangle 8½" × 12½" (21.5 × 31.5 cm) and 1 rectangle 8½" × 6½" (21.5 × 16.5 cm)

▷ Row 5: 1 rectangle 8½" × 2½" (21.5 × 6.5 cm) and 1 rectangle 8½" × 16½" (21.5 × 42 cm).

PREPARE THE APPLIQUÉS

3 • Trace the white portions of the Cups, Pot, Compote, and Pitcher patterns onto the paper side of the fusible web. Trace the 3 white sections of the Vase separately and the 2 Cups separately, including the underlaps indicated by gray lines. Cut out the centers of each piece, leaving at least ¼" (6 mm) around the perimeters and fuse to the white fabric wrong side. Cut the shapes on the drawn lines. Trace the detail shapes for each block onto the paper side of the fusible web, then fuse to the wrong sides of the desired scraps, fussy cutting as desired (page 23).

4 • With a copy of the block pattern right side down on a light box, position the detail pieces on the white vessel piece. Fuse the pieces in place. Do not remove the release paper from the fusible on the main vessel shapes yet, and leave the 2 Cup shapes separate from each other. Repeat this step to fuse all detail pieces to the corresponding vessel shapes. The detail pieces of the Vase will join the white pieces to make a single unit.

APPLIQUÉ AND EMBROIDER THE BLOCKS

5 • Sew around the interior detail pieces with a zigzag stitch (page 37) using matching thread. The detail band on the Pitcher was sewn instead with a scallop stitch along the top and bottom; feel free to use other decorative stitches as desired. The outer side edges of the vessel pieces will be stitched when they're sewn to the background.

6 • Add the stitched details where indicated on the patterns, or as desired (page 42). Sew a straight stitch with white thread down the

variations

A machine blanket stitch could be used around the appliqués, just as you could experiment with other decorative machine stitches to add detail. With some alterations to the preparation steps, this would be a pretty easy quilt to hand-appliqué, perhaps replacing the decorative machine stitches with hand embroidery. Of course, you could make your own version of this quilt in a totally different theme rather than pottery and dishes—maybe zoo animals or holiday prints. Draw your own appliqué patterns for the solid sections, taking ideas from the print fabrics.

center of each detail piece on the Cups and a ball stitch in contrasting thread along each dashed line marked on the Pot pattern.

7 • Position each vessel shape on the appropriate Background, placing it about 1" (2.5 cm) from the bottom and nearest side edge (see Assembly Diagram, page 65), and fuse in place. Make sure to place the partial cup under the full one for the Cups

block. Zigzag around the outer edges of all appliqués, making sure to also sew the inside edges of the handles on the Cups and Pitcher.

ASSEMBLE THE QUILT

8 • Referring to the Assembly Diagram, arrange the blocks and print pieces on a design wall or other flat work surface.

9 • Sew the blocks in each row together. Press the seam allowances toward the solid appliqué backgrounds.

10 • Pin adjacent rows together in sections: sew Rows 1, 2, and 3, then Rows 4 and 5. Pin and sew the 2 sections together.

QUILT AND FINISH
I free-motion quilted around the appliqués to define their edges, then raised the feed dogs and quilted the background with roughly parallel straight lines. I didn't use a quilting guide and instead allowed the lines to be unevenly spaced and a little wobbly, reflecting the more casual edges of the appliqué shapes and the fabric prints that inspired them.

11 • Baste the backing, batting, and quilt top together. Quilt as desired. Trim the excess batting and backing and square the edges of the quilt when finished.

12 • From binding fabric, cut 4 strips 2" (5 cm) × width of fabric. Join the binding strips with diagonal seams and press in half wrong sides together. Bind the quilt.

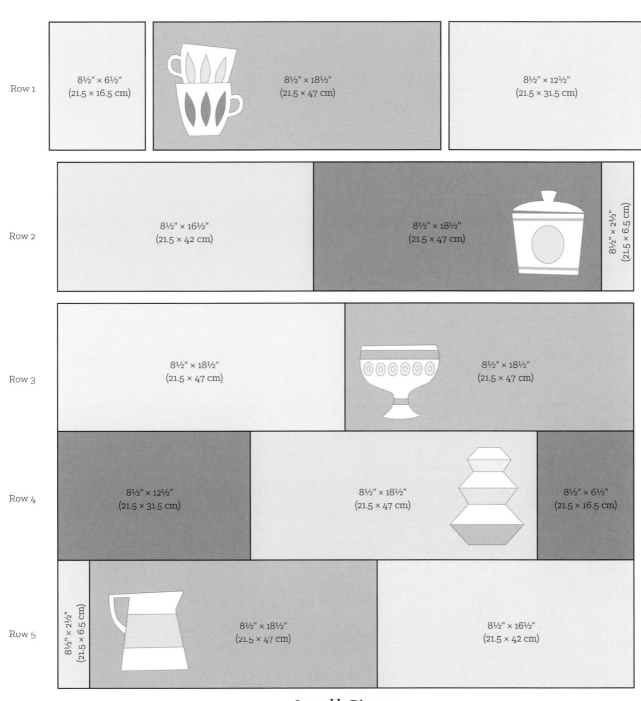

Assembly Diagram

Row 1

8½" × 6½"
(21.5 × 16.5 cm)

8½" × 18½"
(21.5 × 47 cm)

8½" × 12½"
(21.5 × 31.5 cm)

Row 2

8½" × 16½"
(21.5 × 42 cm)

8½" × 18½"
(21.5 × 47 cm)

8½" × 2½"
(21.5 × 6.5 cm)

Row 3

8½" × 18½"
(21.5 × 47 cm)

8½" × 18½"
(21.5 × 47 cm)

Row 4

8½" × 12½"
(21.5 × 31.5 cm)

8½" × 18½"
(21.5 × 47 cm)

8½" × 6½"
(21.5 × 16.5 cm)

Row 5

8½" × 2½"
(21.5 × 6.5 cm)

8½" × 18½"
(21.5 × 47 cm)

8½" × 16½"
(21.5 × 42 cm)

PREPARED-EDGE APPLIQUÉ

If you want to be sure of crisp finished edges before you ever sew a stitch, prepared-edge appliqué is for you. Using a template or other tool, you'll turn the seam allowances to the wrong side of the appliqué with perfect precision.

why prepared-edge appliqué?

Turning edges under before sewing them to a background eliminates the surprise element of sewing pieces down: glued-up blocks look just like the finished product will, making prepared-edge appliqué a what-you-see-is-what-you-get method.

There are many variations on preparing edges for appliqué; the starch-turn method I prefer uses freezer-paper templates with spray starch to hold the seam allowances. I especially like this technique for large appliqués, such as those in the Counterbalance Quilt (page 88), and for highly geometric shapes, such as the circles in the Pineapple Rings Lap Quilt (page 82). But with a little dexterity in manipulating an iron, it works well for even the tiniest shapes.

Bias-tape makers are also invaluable for turning under the edges of long fabric strips to be appliquéd in a structured pattern such as the Cordova Table Runner (page 94) or wandering lines as on the Helix Table Topper (page 98). They can even be combined with freezer-paper templates as for the Counterbalance.

tools and supplies

Prepared-Edge Appliqué at a Glance

TOOLBOX

- Freezer paper and/or bias-tape makers
- Spray starch or spray sizing and brush
- Iron
- Stiletto
- Basting glue
- Scissors
- Needles
- Thread
- Open-toe presser foot and/or narrow-edge presser foot (for machine methods)

PATTERNS AND TEMPLATES

- Use reversed pattern to trace shapes onto freezer paper.
- Use non-reversed pattern to arrange shapes on background.
- Templates have no seam allowances; add seam allowances when cutting fabric.

Prepared-edge appliqué requires more tools than some other methods, but you can pick up several of them on your next trip to the supermarket!

FREEZER PAPER

Freezer paper makes excellent templates over which to turn the edges of appliqué shapes. Doubling the freezer paper for a sturdier template allows the shapes to be used several times before their edges or adhesion wears out, saving work if you're cutting several of the same shape.

STARCH OR SIZING

Spray starch applied to the seam allowances holds the crisp turned edge even after the template is removed. Spray the starch into the bottle's cap or another dish and let the foam settle into a liquid form before using. I brush this on with a stencil brush, but any

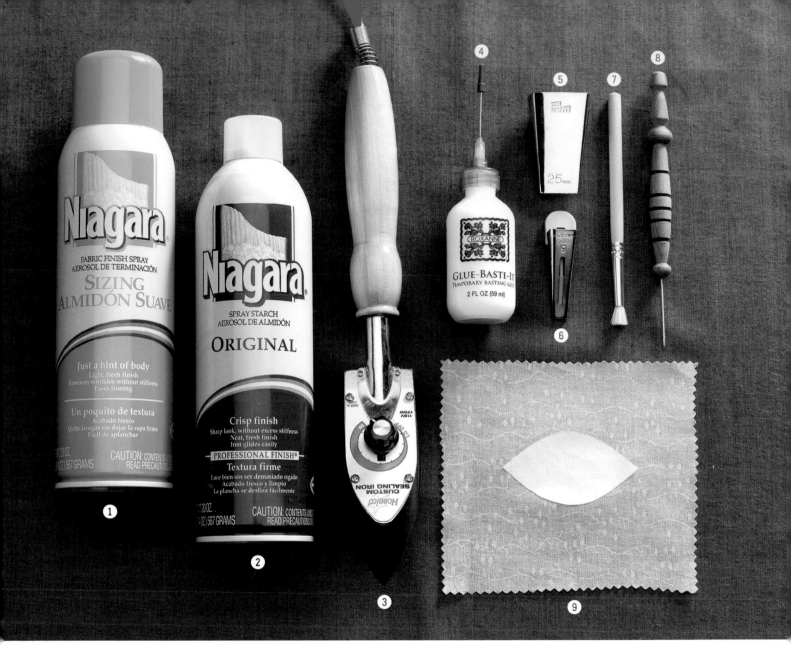

small paintbrush or, in a pinch, even your finger will do. Spray sizing can be used instead of starch—it doesn't leave the flaky residue that heavy applications of starch can, but I find it can degrade the freezer paper faster.

PRESSING TOOLS

Any iron does the job of pressing the edges of the fabric over the template, but a small, maneuverable iron is best. Craft or hobby irons and travel-size irons are good options—being able to attain a high heat is a must,

but the exact model depends on what shape, size, and weight gives you the best control. If you use this method a lot, the starch can discolor your ironing surface over time, so work on an ironing-board cover you're not worried about or protect the surface with a non-stick pressing sheet or parchment paper.

With the iron in one hand, a tool to help manipulate the fabric keeps your fingers out of harm's way. A stiletto is perfect, though I've often gotten away with using a tailor's awl.

Tools and supplies for prepared-edge appliqué:
❶ Sizing; ❷ Spray starch; ❸ Craft iron; ❹ Basting glue; ❺❻ Bias-tape makers; ❼ Stencil brush; ❽ Stiletto; ❾ Freezer-paper template on wrong side of fabric.

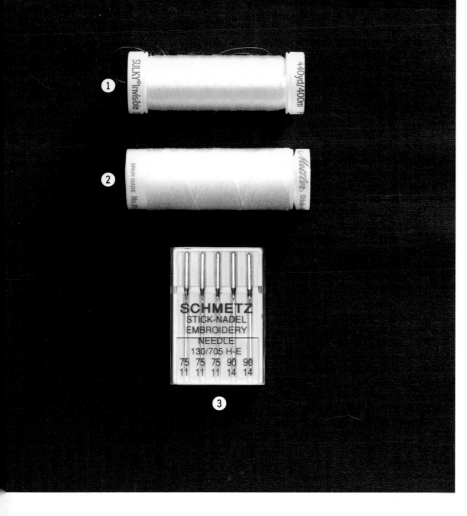

NEEDLES AND THREAD

Invisible machine appliqué requires mono-filament thread, usually clear but also available in darker smoke colors that may hide better on darker fabrics. This extremely fine thread—usually only .004 mm thick—virtually disappears on the appliqué surface. Look for a quality brand that feels soft rather than crispy. Polyester and nylon versions are available; I prefer polyester because it's more resistant to heat, such as that generated by an iron. Use the finest needle you can find in your machine, preferably size 60/8 but no larger than 75/11.

When using monofilament in the top of your machine, a fine sewing thread should be used in the bobbin. I like size 60 machine-embroidery cotton for this, in a color as closely matching the background fabric as I can find. Resist the temptation to use monofilament thread in the bobbin—some types could potentially damage your machine.

For topstitched edges, a regular sewing thread works well, or use a heavier thread for a thicker, more prominent line. A topstitching needle helps keep the stitches perfectly straight.

As for raw-edge appliqué, an open-toe presser foot gives a clear view of the fabric edge in relation to the needle. The centered guide blade of a narrow-edge foot can be used to keep topstitching a consistent distance from the appliqué's edge.

For sewing prepared-edge appliqués by hand, appropriate threads and needles are essentially the same as for needle-turn appliqué. I like fine silk thread that disappears into the fabric, but see page 106 for other options.

Needles and thread for invisible machine appliqué: **❶** Monofilament thread; **❷** Fine cotton thread for bobbin; **❸** Machine-embroidery needles.

BIAS-TAPE MAKERS

For narrow strips of fabric, skip the freezer paper and use a bias-tape maker with the appropriate finished width (which is often engraved, measured in millimeters, on the tape maker). The manufacturer's instructions should tell you how wide to cut strips of fabric to pull through the tape maker for perfect turned-edge strips. Cut fabric on the bias for strips that need to curve; strips cut on the straight grain can be used in areas that don't have curves.

BASTING GLUE

Basting glue holds the appliqués in place until you sew them down. You can glue up a whole block of fiddly little pieces before sewing a stitch.

techniques

Prepare and sew your appliqués following these general guidelines. The project instructions will indicate variations on the procedures where necessary.

TRANSFERRING PATTERNS WITH FREEZER-PAPER TEMPLATES

The shiny plastic side of freezer paper is the side that will stick to fabric if pressed (or melt onto your iron if touched directly)—always place this side against the surface to be adhered.

1 • Place a single layer of freezer paper dull side up over the pattern or template. (Use a light box or bright window if it's difficult to see the pattern lines, but freezer paper is usually thin enough to trace unaided.) Trace each shape needed onto the freezer paper with a pencil **(fig. 1)**, leaving a little space between shapes. Label the shapes if necessary to avoid confusion.

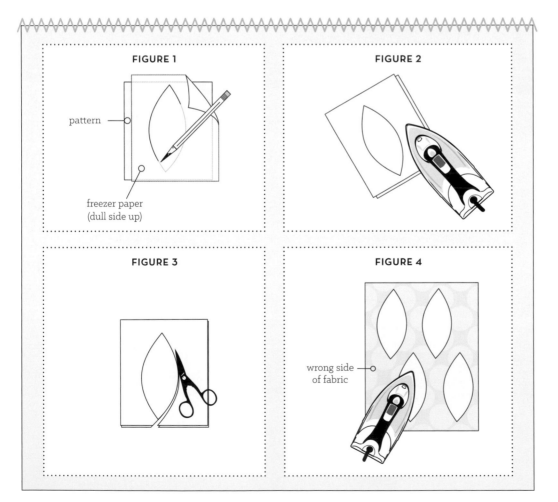

FIGURE 1

pattern

freezer paper
(dull side up)

FIGURE 2

FIGURE 3

FIGURE 4

wrong side
of fabric

▲ *Freezer-paper templates ensure the Counterbalance Quilt's (page 88) appliqués have smooth, symmetrical curves.*

2 • Layer the tracings on a second layer of freezer paper, both dull sides up, on your ironing board. Press with a hot, dry iron to adhere the layers together **(fig. 2)**. Let cool, then peel the doubled freezer paper off the ironing board.

3 • Cut out the shapes from the doubled freezer paper along the traced lines **(fig. 3)**.

4 • Press the freezer-paper templates to the wrong side of your chosen fabric **(fig. 4)**, leaving at least ½" (1.3 cm) between templates. Let cool.

5 • Cut out each shape ³⁄₁₆" to ¼" (5 to 6 mm) beyond the edges of the freezer paper to allow for turn-under **(fig. 5)**. Do not remove the freezer-paper templates.

TURNING EDGES OVER FREEZER PAPER

1 • With a prepared appliqué freezer-paper side up on your ironing board, brush starch or sizing onto several inches of the extended seam allowance **(fig. 6)**.

2 • Fold the starched seam allowance over the freezer-paper template. Press it dry with the tip of your iron, holding the seam allowance in place with a stiletto ahead of the iron to keep it tight around the template's edge **(fig. 7)**.

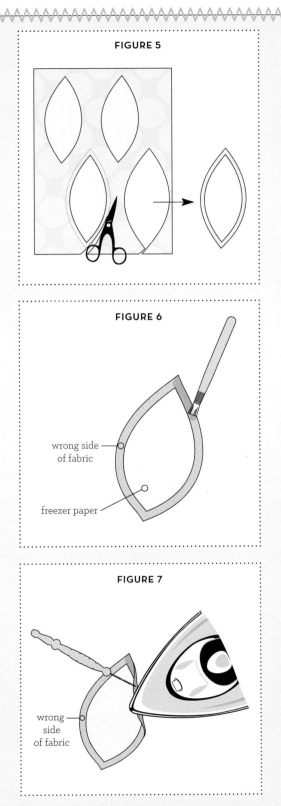

FIGURE 5

FIGURE 6

wrong side of fabric

freezer paper

FIGURE 7

wrong side of fabric

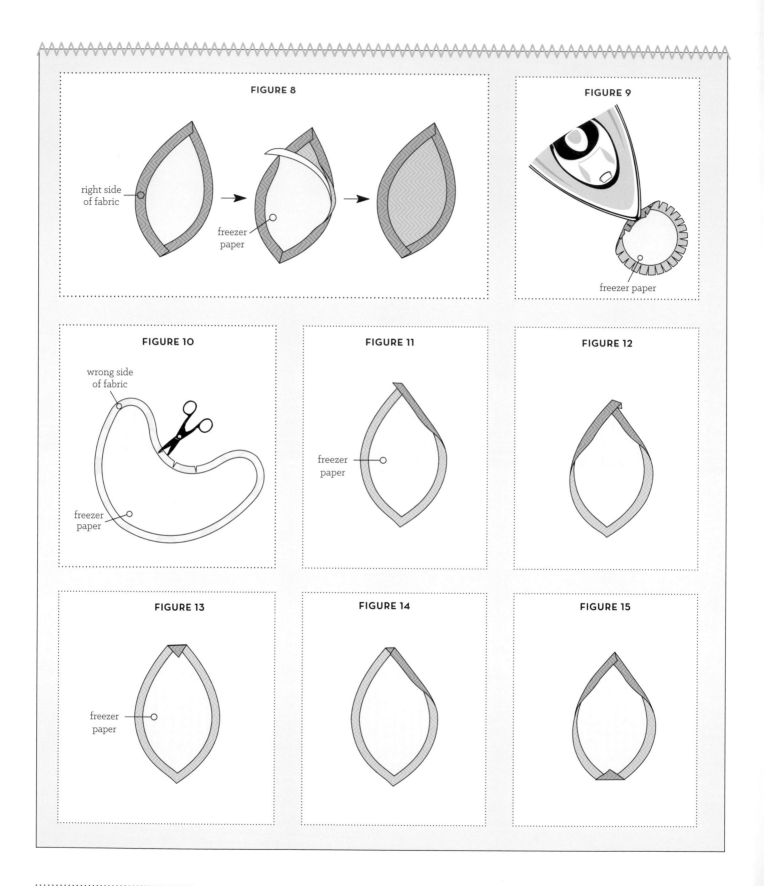

FIGURE 8

right side
of fabric

freezer
paper

FIGURE 9

freezer paper

FIGURE 10

wrong side
of fabric

freezer
paper

FIGURE 11

freezer
paper

FIGURE 12

FIGURE 13

freezer
paper

FIGURE 14

FIGURE 15

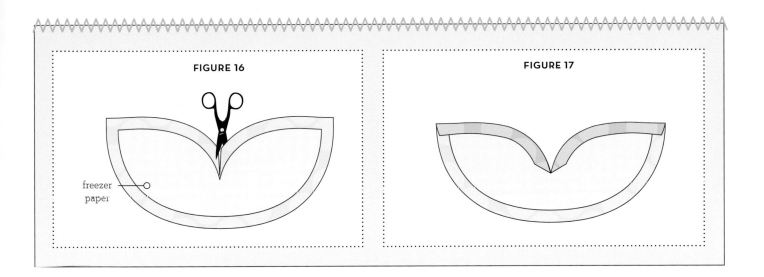

FIGURE 16

freezer paper

FIGURE 17

3 • Brush starch onto another several inches of seam allowance, then iron it over the template edge, and continue this process all the way around the shape. When cool, lift the seam allowances to peel away the freezer paper template—the edges will retain their pressed shape **(fig. 8)**.

Dealing with Outside Curves

Extremely tight curves—such as tiny circles—may need to have their seam allowances clipped to eliminate bulk **(fig. 9)**, but I rarely clip, instead relying on bias stretch and starch to press the seam allowances into submission. Cutting the fabric outside the template with pinking shears instead of regular scissors can also reduce bulk in curved seam allowances.

Dealing with Inside Curves

Clipping the seam allowances is needed more often for concave (inside) curves than for convex (outside) curves; make sure to snip only to within a couple threads of the freezer-paper template **(fig. 10)**. Again, I don't really bother unless absolutely necessary—if the seam allowance is pulled out of shape but isn't taut around the edge of the template, a snip at the center of the curve will release the tension and let the seam allowance spread where it needs to.

Dealing with Outside Points

Either press over the seam allowance to one side of the point and then the other **(figs. 11 and 12)**, or press the point's seam allowance over first, then the two sides **(figs. 13–15)**. If you don't press the point down first, you'll need to tuck the dog-ear under while you're sewing.

Dealing with Inside Corners

Clip the seam allowance up to the corner, but stop just short of cutting through the freezer-paper template **(fig. 16)**. Press over the seam allowance to both sides of the corner **(fig. 17)**, taking extra care to keep the narrower seam allowances near the corner taut around the template. The starch should give the fabric enough stability to keep it from fraying at the corner point, but if it does start to ravel, dab the corner sparingly with fray preventer and press dry, making sure the seam allowances remain taut.

TURNING EDGES WITH BIAS-TAPE MAKERS

Strips of a consistent width are easy to prepare with bias-tape makers, available in a variety of finished widths. Strips cut on the fabric's straight grain are fine if the finished strips don't need to bend or curve (as in the Counterbalance Quilt, page 88), but you'll need strips cut on the bias (diagonal) if they have to go around any curves. A light application of spray starch can ease the fabric through the bias-tape maker if you have trouble.

1 · Cut strips of fabric as indicated by the project instructions. The cut widths for bias-maker strips given in this book are common, but double-check with the instructions that came with your bias-tape maker to be sure you're cutting the correct width.

2 · If you need lengths of bias tape longer than your fabric will allow, piece multiple strips together with a diagonal seam to distribute the bulk. For straight-grain strips with square ends, crease one end of the top strip on the diagonal **(fig. 18)**, line it up with the bottom strip at right angles (right sides together), sew along the crease **(fig. 19)**, then trim the excess fabric to leave a ¼" (6 mm) seam allowance. For bias strips with angled ends, put the ends right sides together at right angles, with the angled edges flush and corners extending so the intersection of the strips is lined up to sew with a ¼" (6 mm) seam allowance, then sew **(fig. 20)**. Press the seam allowances open and trim any dog-ears.

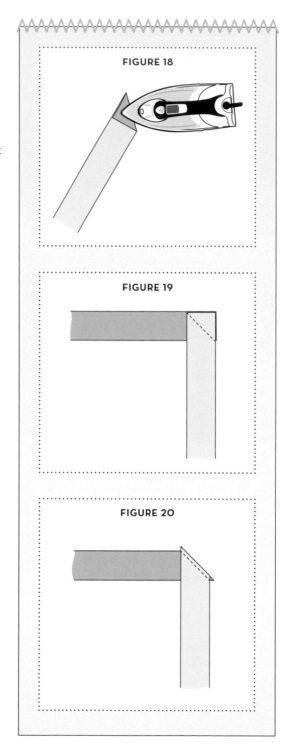

FIGURE 18

FIGURE 19

FIGURE 20

◀ *Some projects require only short lengths of bias tape, so you won't need to piece the strips first. The instructions for the Cordova Table Runner (page 94) give the exact size you'll need for short individual strips.*

3 • Referring to the bias-tape maker's instructions, feed the strip of fabric into the wide end, using a stiletto or long pin to help pull the fabric through to the narrow end. (Straight-grain strips are easier to start if you trim the starting end on an angle.) Pull 1" (2.5 cm) or so from the narrow end of the tape maker, raw edges up, and press to secure the folds created by the tape maker.

4 • Pull the bias-tape maker along the unfolded strip length **(fig. 21)**, following with the iron to press the folds. When the entire length has been folded and pressed into a strip of the required width, you're ready to use it in your project.

❀ *tip*

Short lengths of leftover bias tape are perfect to use when testing tension and other sewing machine settings, since it's important that any test have the same layers as real appliqué.

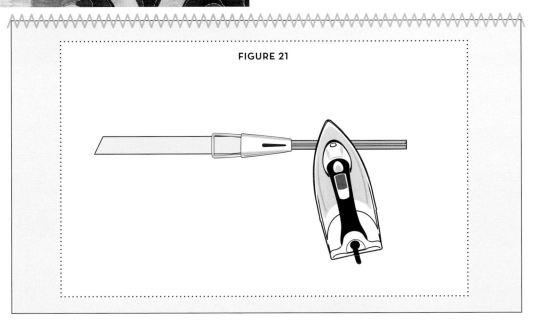

FIGURE 21

GLUING UP BLOCKS

I usually use this no-mark light-box method, but for dark backgrounds or blocks with lots of appliqué layers, tracing or an overlay may be useful (see page 22). Make sure you've removed any freezer-paper templates from the appliqués. If the pieces are numbered on the pattern, start with number 1 and work sequentially.

1 • Place the pattern on a light box so it "reads" in the finished direction. Place the background fabric right side up on top **(fig. 22)**, aligning any guide marks as described in the instructions. (Appliqué patterns commonly show the vertical and horizontal centerlines for orientation; lightly press the background in half both ways and align the creases with the centerlines.)

2 • Position the lowermost appliqué piece on the background fabric where the shape appears on the pattern. Carefully keeping the appliqué in place, lift the edges to dab small dots of basting glue on the turned-under seam allowance **(fig. 23)**, and apply slight pressure with your fingers to adhere to the background. Large pieces need only a dot of glue every 1" (2.5 cm) or so, or about as frequently as you'd pin. Remember that the glue is just for basting; it doesn't need to be welded down permanently.

3 • Continue positioning and glue-basting appliqué pieces in sequence, working toward the uppermost layer of appliqué **(fig. 24)**. Trace any embroidery lines onto the fabric before removing it from the pattern.

SEWING BY HAND (WITH A BLINDSTITCH)

The blindstitch described here is basic to much hand appliqué, including needle-turn (page 110). Keeping the stitches hidden but secure is more important than exact stitch length, but try to keep stitches no longer than 1⁄16" (2 mm). Sew from the lowermost layer up. Overlapped sections of fabric don't need to be sewn down.

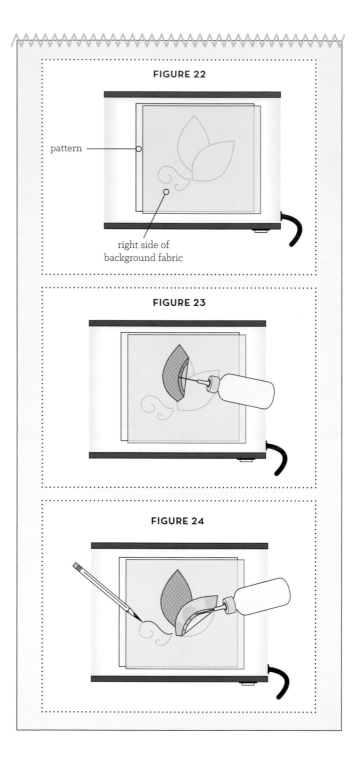

FIGURE 22

pattern

right side of
background fabric

FIGURE 23

FIGURE 24

1 · Knot the thread and bring the needle out through the folded edge of the appliqué fabric, toward the bottom of the fold. It's easiest to start sewing at a gently curved section of the appliqué, rather than at a corner.

2 · Take the needle through the background fabric immediately next to where it emerged from the appliqué and bring it back through the folded edge at most 1⁄16" (2 mm) ahead of the previous stitch **(fig. 25)**. Try to keep slightly to the side of the fold nearest the background to help hide the stitches.

3 · Continue sewing as described until you've sewn all the way around the shape. Most challenging areas (curves, points, etc.) have already been tamed when turning the edges; make sure to take a stitch at the very tip of sharp points and use an extra stitch or two to secure sharp inside corners.

4 · When finished, knot the thread off on the back of the work.

SEWING BY MACHINE

With invisible machine appliqué, sometimes called mock hand appliqué, monofilament thread secures the appliqué edges but remains virtually invisible, especially when you step back from the sewing machine to a more normal viewing distance. A blind-hem stitch is usually recommended, though a zigzag stitch can be used instead. The choice of stitch is largely dependent on how much control your sewing machine gives you: neither of my machines has a blind hem perfectly suited to appliqué, so I've given up trying to force the issue. My machines give me more control over their zigzags, and since that's the case for a wider range of sewing machines, I'll give the most detail for invisible appliqué by zigzag stitch here.

For a quicker, more visible approach, consider topstitching.

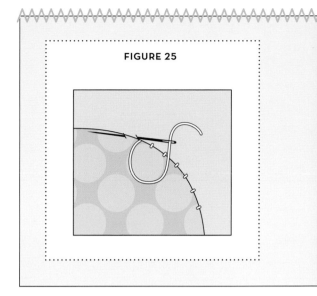

FIGURE 25

Zigzag Stitch

Navigate around curves, corners, and points as for raw-edge zigzag stitch (pages 38–41). Stitch width and other settings are suggestions for starting points, but make adjustments to find what works best for your fabric, machine, and threads—you may want to make a note of these settings for future reference.

1 · Thread the sewing machine with monofilament thread and install a bobbin filled with size 60 cotton thread. Install a size 60/8 needle and an open-toe presser foot, if available. Engage the needle-down function, if available.

2 · Set the machine for a zigzag stitch about 1 mm long and 1 mm wide. Sew a sample on scraps of similar fabric (including a turned-appliqué edge) and adjust the tension so the bobbin thread does not show on the right side. The size 60/8 needle will help prevent the bobbin thread from showing, but if tension adjustments can't completely hide it, the dots of bobbin thread can at least be camouflaged if the thread color matches the background.

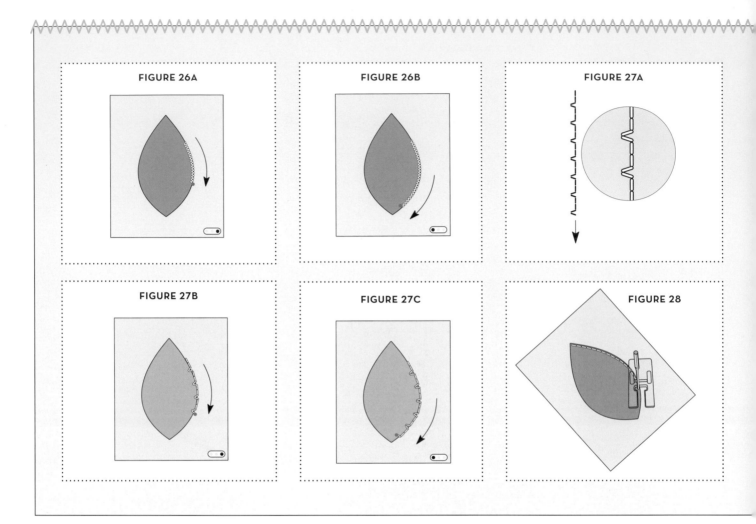

FIGURE 26A

FIGURE 26B

FIGURE 27A

FIGURE 27B

FIGURE 27C

FIGURE 28

3 • Place the work right side up under the presser foot and lower the needle partway. Position the work so the needle will enter the background fabric just to the side of the appliqué (the needle should be on the outer swing when starting). Lower the presser foot, hold both top and bobbin threads, and take a stitch or two. The outer swing of the needle should continue to just graze the appliqué fabric but not catch it, while the inner swing catches a couple threads of the appliqué fabric. Let go of the threads and continue sewing with the needle's outer swing following the outside edge of the appliqué **(figs. 26a and 26b)**.

Blind-Hem Stitch

A machine blind-hem stitch makes several straight stitches, then "bites" to the left and back before making a further set of straight stitches. This can be perfect for invisible machine appliqué, depending on how your machine executes the stitch and what control it allows you: the blind hem on one of my machines has too many straight stitches between the bites, and my other machine won't let me set the width narrow enough. The ideal is two straight stitches between the bites **(fig. 27a)**, allowing the straight stitches to be longer than pinpricks with the bites ⅛" (3 mm) apart at most. The width

▲ *On the right swing, the needle falls just outside the appliqué (fig. 26a). On the left swing, the needle falls a couple threads inside the appliqué (fig. 26b).*

On the right swing, the needle falls just to the side of the appliqué, making straight stitches (fig. 27b). On the left swing of the needle, a bite is made into the appliqué (fig. 27c).

✿ *tip*

At some point, your mind or machine will wander from the edge of the appliqué slightly, leaving a gap in the stitching that holds it to the background. Resewing by machine leaves more ends of monofilament thread to secure, so I find it easier to just thread a needle and sew these gaps down by hand.

of the bite should, like the zigzag stitch described above, be just enough to land a couple threads into the appliqué **(figs. 27b and 27c)**. The general procedure is similar to invisible appliqué with a zigzag stitch. More detail on using a blind-hem stitch for invisible machine appliqué is covered by some excellent books listed in the Resources section, but I've been pleasantly surprised at the effectiveness of a zigzag for the same technique.

Topstitch

Topstitching the edges rather than zigzagging over them gives the appliqués a little extra dimension: since the extreme edges are free of the background fabric, they float a little about the quilted background. It's also a quicker and more forgiving technique, since you don't need to be as precise about guiding the needle around the edge. Set the stitch length for 2.5 to 3 mm (or longer for heavier threads) and sew straight stitches about ⅛" (3 mm) from the edge **(fig. 28)**. Guide the stitching with the inside of the toe on a ¼" (6 mm) presser foot or the blade of a narrow-edge foot to maintain a consistent distance from the edge. Secure the ends of the thread with backstitching or by tying them together on the back of the work. If your appliqué shapes have corners, shorten the stitch length as you approach the corners, if necessary, to keep the stitches on the other side of the corner a consistent distance from the edge.

Note that a wider seam allowance is used when cutting out the appliqués for the Pineapple Rings Lap Quilt (page 82), the project in this chapter that uses topstitching. This extra room ensures the stitches will catch both the front of the appliqué and the turned-under seam allowance, since most topstitching is farther in from the edge than other prepared-edge stitches.

Securing Ends of Monofilament Thread

Monofilament thread is meant to be invisible, so it's a bit of a challenge to thread loose ends through a hand needle to take them to the back of the work, as I suggest for a raw-edge zigzag. Backstitching gives too much opportunity for imperfect tension that will pull bobbin thread to the front. Wherever possible, I start and stop invisible machine appliqué where subsequent seams will secure the appliqué stitches: for the bias strips in the Cordova Table Runner (page 94), I start in the seam allowances of the block backgrounds, since these will be joined to the sashing strips; for Counterbalance (page 88), the binding secures stitching that starts and ends around the quilt's perimeter. Where this isn't possible, I usually make do with backstitching or start and end by dropping the stitch length down to almost zero and sewing a few straight stitches.

PINEAPPLE RINGS LAP QUILT

APPLIQUÉ TECHNIQUE
Starch-turned, prepared-edge appliqué with prepieced shapes and topstitched edges

FINISHED SIZE
48" × 60" (122 × 152.5 cm)

MATERIALS
- ○ 2½ yd (2.3 m) white solid fabric for backgrounds

- ○ 3⅛ yd (2.86 m) total assorted yellow and white prints for ring wedges; if using scraps, each should be at least 4" × 4¼" (10 × 11.5 cm)

- ○ 3⅛ yd (2.86 m) backing fabric

- ○ ½ yd (45.5 cm) binding fabric

- ○ 56" × 68" (142 × 172.7 cm) batting

TOOLS
- ○ Pinking shears

- ○ 30-degree wedge ruler (optional)

- ○ Ring and Wedge templates (pattern insert B)

- ○ Toolbox for prepared-edge appliqué (page 69)

If you're a patchworker wary of making the jump to appliqué, this quilt should only slightly nudge you out of your comfort zone—you don't even have to take your machine off straight stitch to sew the topstitched edges! It almost feels like cheating to describe the quilt as appliquéd—there's actually more piecing in it than there is appliqué. But far from cheating, appliquéing pieces of fabric that have first been pieced together is the best of both worlds. The more techniques you know, the more you can combine them to make your work easier or more interesting.

choosing fabric

A monochromatic palette need not be boring. My main rule for picking fabric for Pineapple Rings was that the pattern be white on yellow, although "yellow" is a range more than an absolute hue here. Fabrics that were too orange or too green compared to the others were left out, but a few of the prints are accented with deeper gold or even green; limited to one or two wedges per block, they prevent the quilt from looking washed out.

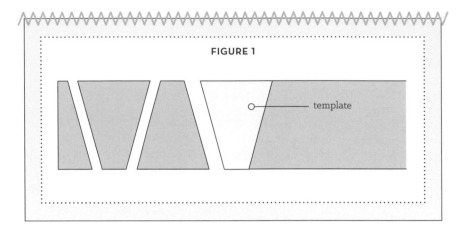

FIGURE 1

template

CUT THE FABRIC

1 • From white solid fabric, cut:

▷ 20 Background squares 12½" × 12½" (31.5 × 31.5 cm).

2 • Using the Wedge template (or a specialized ruler; see Cutting Wedges on the opposite page), cut a total of 240 Wedges (12 per block) from the yellow prints. You may find it helpful to cut 4½" (11.5 cm) wide strips of the fabric first, then use the template to cut the strip into Wedges **(fig. 1)**.

PREPARE THE RINGS

3 • Transfer the Ring template onto doubled freezer paper, including the guidelines, and cut out a template. Cut out the center hole.

4 • Split a group of 12 Wedges into 2 groups of 6, mixing assorted prints. Piece each group together along the long edges to make 2 semicircles. Press the seam allowances open, then pin the semicircles right sides together and sew them into a ring shape, again pressing the seam allowances open **(fig. 2)**.

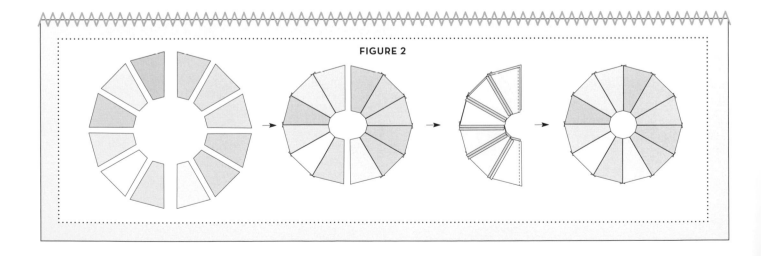

FIGURE 2

5 • Aligning the guidelines of the freezer-paper Ring template with 4 of the seams, press the Ring template to the wrong side of the seamed Wedges. (It doesn't matter which particular seams you align; lining up any 4 of them just makes sure the template is properly centered on the fabric.) Trim around the fabric outer edge with pinking shears, leaving a seam allowance of about ¼" (6 mm) to prevent raveling and to help distribute the bulk of the seam allowance when turned over the template. Around the inside edge, clip into the seam allowance once or twice for each Wedge, clipping almost to the template.

6 • Starch and press the outer edges of the fabric over the template (see page 73), taking care to keep the curved edge smooth at the seams. Starch and press the inner edges over the template, then remove the template. Repeat Steps 4 to 6 to prepare a total of 20 Rings.

APPLIQUÉ THE RINGS

7 • Lightly press a Background square in half both ways to mark the center. Place a prepared Ring right side up on the Background, aligning 4 of the Ring seams with the creases in the Background. (Again, it doesn't matter which seams you align, unless you want to position certain wedges specifically, like making sure they're at the top of the block.) Glue-baste (page 78) the Ring to the Background.

8 • Topstitch the Ring to the Background square (page 81) ⅛" (3 mm) from both the inner and outer edges. Repeat Steps 7 and 8 to make a total of 20 blocks.

ASSEMBLE THE QUILT

9 • Arrange the blocks on a design wall or other flat work surface in 5 rows of 4 blocks each. The specific placement isn't crucial if your Wedge fabrics are all similar in color as in the sample quilt; I just made sure the same prints didn't habitually appear in the same position in several blocks, and I tried to distribute the Wedges that had slightly darker values so they didn't cluster together.

10 • Sew each row of blocks together. Press the seam allowances to one side, alternating the direction for adjacent rows.

Cutting Wedges

Instead of using the Wedge template, you could use a ruler designed for cutting 30-degree wedges. If you're not sure of a ruler's angle measurement, check it against the template on pattern insert B. The ruler will likely be longer than the template, and it may come to a sharper point, but it will work if you can get the two angled edges to match; just make sure to position the ruler on the fabric so the shape you cut is the same size as the Wedge template. The ruler manufacturer's instructions may be helpful.

Tools Rule

Craft stores carry a wide range of circle-cutting tools in the scrapbooking section, and they can be very useful for making precise freezer-paper templates. The Ring template used here is simply an 11" (28 cm) diameter circle with a 4" (10 cm) hole removed from the center.

11 • Pin adjacent rows together in sections, aligning the seam allowances; sew Rows 1, 2, and 3, then Rows 4 and 5. Pin and sew the 2 sections together.

QUILT AND FINISH

All the quilting for the sample was done free-motion on a domestic sewing machine. The white background, including the ring centers, was filled with a simple meander, and the ring shapes were emphasized by quilting around the outer and inner edges. The shape of each wedge was echoed once inside the seams. I used white thread to do all the quilting on the white sections before switching to a yellow thread to quilt the rings themselves.

12 • Cut the backing fabric into 2 equal lengths. Sew these sections together with a horizontal seam to make a backing at least 56" × 68" (142 × 172.7 cm).

13 • Baste the backing, batting, and quilt top together. Quilt as desired. Trim the excess batting and backing and square the edges of the quilt when finished.

14 • From binding fabric, cut 6 strips 2" (5 cm) × width of fabric. Join the binding strips with diagonal seams, and press in half wrong sides together. Bind the quilt.

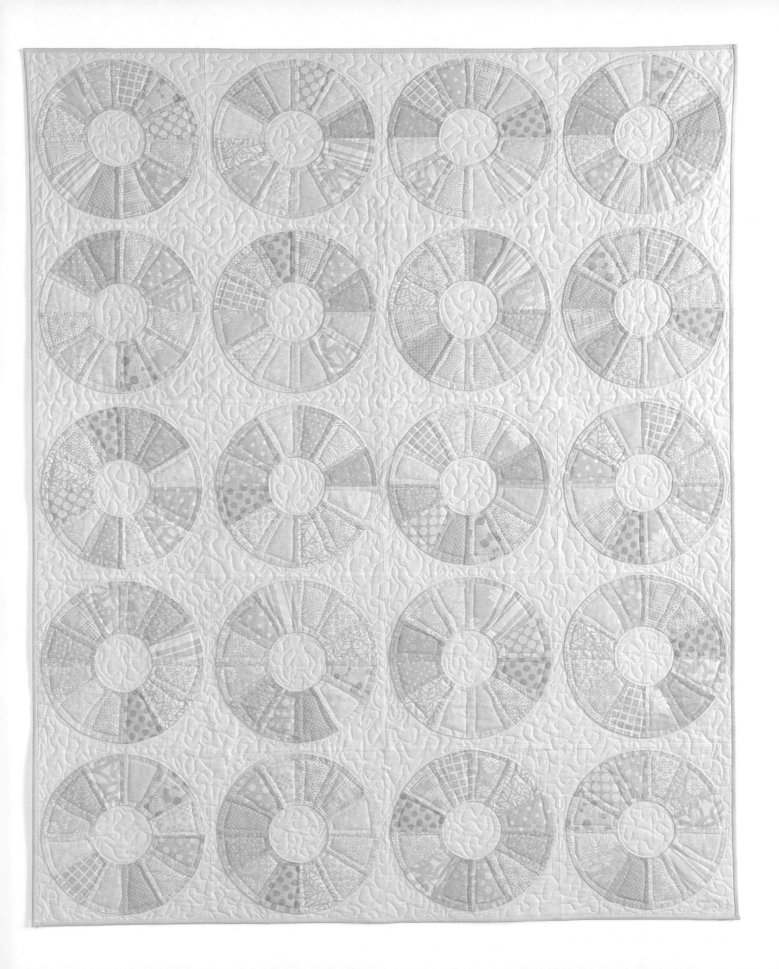

COUNTER-BALANCE QUILT

APPLIQUÉ TECHNIQUE
Invisible machine appliqué with prepared edges

FINISHED SIZE
80" × 90" (203 × 228.6 cm); to fit a full- or queen-size bed

MATERIALS

○ 5¼ yd (4.8 m) chartreuse solid fabric for background

○ ½ yd (45.5 cm) each of 7 gray tonal prints

○ 5½ yd (5 m) backing fabric

○ ½ yd (45.5 cm) binding fabric

○ 88" × 98" (223.5 × 248.9 cm) batting

○ ½ yd (45.5 cm) freezer paper

TOOLS

○ 1" (2.5 cm) bias-tape maker

○ Bulb template (pattern insert B)

○ Toolbox for prepared-edge appliqué (page 69)

I love how the simple construction of this quilt imparts a sense of movement. The gray bulb-like shapes feel like they're zipping up and down on the narrow strips, an effect created by balancing them at different levels across the width of the quilt. The quilting reinforces the effect, a good example of how appliqué and quilting can work together toward a design goal. This quilt also ignores the conventional quilt-block structure entirely. Instead, the background is made from two lengths of fabric, with large-scale appliqués sewn directly to them. In less time than it would take to appliqué a detailed quilt block, you can sew up the entire top of this high-impact quilt.

choosing fabric

Modern quilters tend to prefer solid fabrics or designer collections. While I love both, the lowly tone-on-tone print adds an extremely useful middle ground, especially now that manufacturers have branched out beyond the mottled, marbled standbys of years past. As traditional quilters have long known, tonal prints add depth, especially when they're paired with a solid fabric.

CUT THE FABRIC

1 • From chartreuse background fabric, cut:

   ▷ 2 Background rectangles 40½" × 90" (103 × 228.6 cm).

2 • From each gray print, cut:

   ▷ 2 strips 2" (5 cm) (or width directed by tape-maker's instructions) × width of fabric. Trim off the selvedges. (The remaining fabric will be used later for the Bulb shapes.)

MAKE THE BULB STRIPS

3 • The finished Bulb Strips will be about 8" (20.5 cm) longer than the quilt top, so for any Bulbs you want within 8" (20.5 cm) of the quilt top horizontal center, set the corresponding strips aside for now (1 or 2 pairs). Join the remaining pairs of strips together with a diagonal seam to make one long strip of each fabric. Trim the excess fabric and press the seam allowances open.

4 • Run each strip through the bias-tape maker to turn the edges under. The short strips set aside in the previous step should be run through the tape maker, too.

5 • Trace and cut out the Bulb template from doubled freezer paper. Press the freezer-paper template onto the wrong side of the remaining fabric of one of the gray prints. Cut the fabric ¼" (6 mm) beyond the edge of the freezer paper (use an acrylic ruler and rotary cutter to make sure your cut is straight and exactly ¼" [6 mm] past the flat ends of the Bulb).

6 • Starch and press the outer edges of the Bulb fabric over the template along the curved edges, leaving the flat ends unpressed **(fig. 1)**. Remove the template and repeat Steps 5 and 6 with the remaining gray prints to prepare 7 Bulbs, one matching each strip (or pair of short strips).

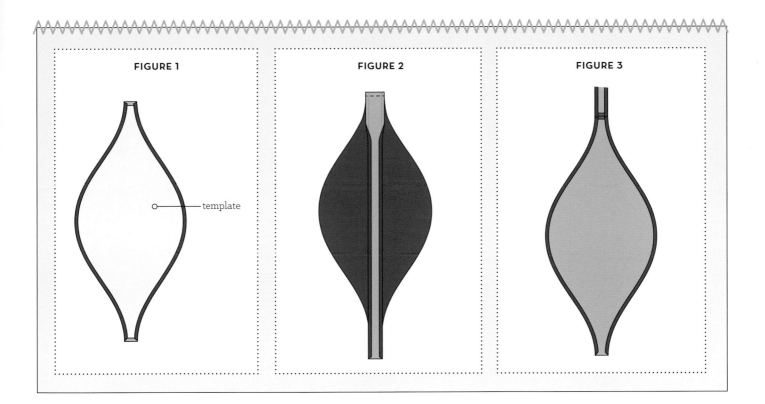

FIGURE 1

template

FIGURE 2

FIGURE 3

7 • Open the folded edges at one end of a Bulb piece and one end of one of the matching short strips. Aligning the raw edges and the creases, pin these pieces right sides together. Keeping the folded edges open, sew with a ¼" (6 mm) seam allowance **(fig. 2)**. Finger-press the seam allowances open, refold the edges, and press flat **(fig. 3)**. The curve of the Bulb should smoothly blend into the straight strip. At the opposite end of the Bulb, repeat this step to join the remaining short strip. Assemble any other short-strip sets the same way.

8 • For the longer strips that have already been joined together, determine where to insert the Bulb. Vary this point so the Bulbs aren't all the same distance from the edge of the quilt. Using an acrylic ruler and rotary cutter, make a straight cut across the strip at the insertion point, then follow Step 7 to sew the ends of the corresponding Bulb to the cut edges of the strip. Repeat until all Bulbs are pieced into a strip.

APPLIQUÉ THE BULB STRIPS

9 • On a design wall or other flat work surface, lay out the Bulb Strips in a sequence you like, balancing shades of gray and position of the Bulbs across the quilt. You'll work from the center out on each of the 2 Background sections, to reduce the amount of fabric handled at one time—the center strip of the quilt will be the last one sewn, joining the 2 sections.

10 • Referring to **fig. 4** on the next page, mark 10½" (26.5 cm) in from one of the long edges of one chartreuse Background piece, down the entire length. Place the right-of-center strip along this line, with the inner edge butted against the line (i.e., the edge of the strip should be 10½" [26.5 cm] from the edge of the Background), glue-basting as you position the strip. The Bulb section, of course, will bulge outside the marked distance; just keep the straight strip sections on the line. Mark another line 9¾" (25 cm) from the outer edge of this strip and glue-baste

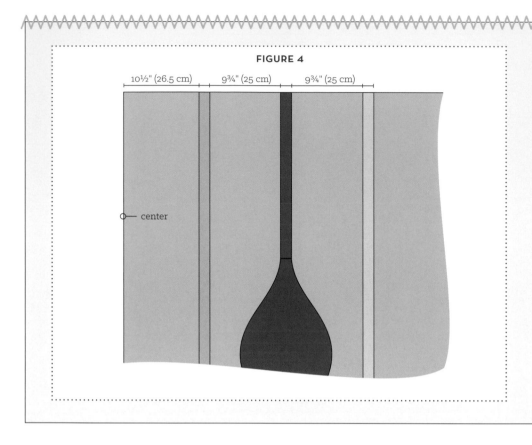

FIGURE 4

10½" (26.5 cm) 9¾" (25 cm) 9¾" (25 cm)

center

variations

While I vertically positioned my bulbs more or less randomly, think about creating patterns, too—try a swath of bulbs rising from one corner to the opposite, either in a straight line or a curve. Or add some extra bulbs so some or all the strips have more than one. If the bulbs themselves are too plain for you, give them some quilted detail, an appliquéd shape in the middle, or even some reverse appliqué to turn them into loops.

the next strip in place at this position. Mark and baste the outermost strip another 9¾" (25 cm) away. Repeat this step to glue-baste the left-of-center strips to the remaining Background piece, working outward in the opposite direction.

11 • Using monofilament thread, sew both edges of each Bulb Strip to the background fabric (page 79).

12 • When each Background piece has its 3 Bulb Strips sewn down, pin the Background pieces right sides together at the center edges. Sew them together and press the seam allowances open. Center the remaining Bulb Strip over the seam and glue-baste it in place. Sew the center Bulb Strip edges as described in Step 11.

QUILT AND FINISH

I kept my feed dogs up and let the walking foot do the work for this one, quilting straight lines parallel to the strips. For 6 lines in each section between strips, the lines were spaced about 1⅜" (3.5 cm) apart (using a quilting guide to measure the distance), but they get closer together near the bulbs, as if the bulbs are forcing the lines apart as they move up and down their strips.

13 • Cut the backing fabric into two 2¾ yd (2.5 m) sections. Sew the sections together with a vertical seam to make a backing at least 88" × 98" (223.5 × 248.9 cm).

14 • Baste the backing, batting, and quilt top together. Quilt as desired. Trim the excess batting and backing (and any excess Bulb Strips), and square the edges of the quilt.

15 • From binding fabric, cut 9 strips 2" (5 cm) wide × width of fabric. Join the binding strips with diagonal seams and press in half wrong sides together. Bind the quilt.

CORDOVA TABLE RUNNER

APPLIQUÉ TECHNIQUE
Invisible machine appliqué with bias strips

FINISHED SIZE
13½" × 39½" (34.5 × 100.5 cm)

MATERIALS
○ ¾ yd (68.5 cm) off-white solid fabric for bias strips, sashing, and binding

○ 12 squares, each 6" × 6" (15 × 15 cm), assorted prints for backgrounds

○ ⅔ yd (61 cm) backing fabric

○ 18" × 44" (45.5 × 112 cm) batting

TOOLS
○ ½" (1.3 cm) bias-tape maker

○ Cordova Block pattern (pattern insert C)

○ Toolbox for prepared-edge appliqué (page 69)

○ Light box (optional)

Perhaps it isn't coincidence that both concrete and quilts come in block form. I was intrigued by the way the separate blocks of concrete walls make circle patterns when put together, just like quilt blocks take on a new life when they interact with copies of themselves in a quilt top. Concrete sellers call the common breeze-block design replicated in this runner Cordova, and since the concrete version is often used to build walls in and around gardens, it seemed only natural to use floral prints as the background fabric.

choosing fabric

Medium- to large-scale prints such as the florals used here demand a place of prominence and lose their effect if chopped up into tiny pieces. By placing them behind the bias strips, they retain their impact, drawing the eye through the bias-strip design in front of them. Landscape architects do this by alternately concealing and revealing glimpses of different settings beyond hedges, fences, or, appropriately enough, perforated concrete walls.

CUT THE FABRIC

1 • From off-white solid fabric, cut:

- ▷ 2 strips 4" (10 cm) × width-of-fabric; sub-cut each 4" (10 cm) strip into 1" (2.5 cm) wide *bias* strips. You'll need a total of 48 bias strips. (You should be able to make a few extra bias strips, which are useful for testing your machine settings before sewing the actual blocks.)
- ▷ 5 Horizontal Sashings 1½" × 12½" (3.8 × 31.5 cm)
- ▷ 6 Vertical Sashings 1½" × 6" (3.8 × 15 cm)
- ▷ 2 Long Borders 1" × 38½" (2.5 × 98 cm)
- ▷ 2 Short Borders 1" × 13½" (2.5 × 34.5 cm).

PREPARE THE BIAS STRIPS

2 • Run each bias strip through the bias-tape maker to turn the edges under to make ½" (1.3 cm) wide finished strips (page 76).

3 • With a copy of the Cordova Block pattern right side up on a light box, place one of the 6" (15 cm) background squares right side up, aligning the edges with the solid square outline. (The dashed line indicates the seam line.)

4 • Position a bias strip on one of the curved sections of the pattern. Starting from one end (leaving a bit of an overhang past the background fabric), glue-baste the bias strip to the background fabric. You'll need to curve the bias strip gradually to follow the pattern lines; the strip should extend a little past the opposite end, too. If the strip ripples instead of lying flat, gently press to relax it. Glue-baste the other 3 strips to the background square where indicated on the pattern. Repeat to make to a total of 12 blocks.

APPLIQUÉ THE BIAS STRIPS

5 • Sew along both curved edges of each bias strip with a zigzag or blind-hem stitch (page 79) using monofilament thread.

6 • Trim the excess bias strip length even with the background squares.

ASSEMBLE THE RUNNER

Note: Press all seam allowances toward the sashing and border strips to help make them look like an extension of the appliqué.

7 • Referring to the Assembly Diagram, arrange the blocks in 6 rows of 2 blocks each on a design wall or other flat work surface.

8 • Join the blocks from each row with a Vertical Sashing strip.

9 • Join adjacent rows with a Horizontal Sashing strip.

10 • Pin and sew a Long Border strip to each long edge of the runner top and press. Sew a Short Border strip to each short edge of the runner top.

QUILT AND FINISH

A table runner is a very manageable size to quilt on a domestic machine. After quilting straight lines down the center of the sashing strips (to make the sashing look more like a border around each block), I switched to free-motion and outlined all the off-white pieces. Taking a cue from the floral prints I used, I quilted a daisy shape in each block center and a quarter daisy in each of the bias-framed quarter circles.

11 • Baste the backing, batting, and runner top together. Quilt as desired. Trim the excess batting and backing and square the edges of the runner.

12 • From the remaining off-white solid fabric, cut 3 strips 2" (5 cm) × width of fabric for binding. Join the binding strips with diagonal seams and press in half wrong sides together. Bind the runner.

1" × 13½"
(2.5 × 34.5 cm)

1½" × 6"
(3.8 × 15 cm)

6" × 6"
(15 × 15 cm)

1" × 38½" (2.5 × 98 cm)

1½" × 12½" (3.8 × 31.5 cm)

Assembly Diagram

HELIX TABLE TOPPER

APPLIQUÉ TECHNIQUE
Improvisational prepared-edge appliqué with handsewn bias strips

FINISHED SIZE
24" (61 cm) diameter

MATERIALS
- ¾ yd (68.5 cm) gray solid fabric for background

- ½ yd (45.5 cm) each of 2 yarn-dyed fabrics for bias strips

- ⅞ yd (80 cm) backing fabric

- 27" x 27" (68.5 x 68.5 cm) batting

TOOLS
- ⅜" (1 cm) bias-tape maker

- Background template (pattern insert C)

- Toolbox for prepared-edge appliqué (page 69)

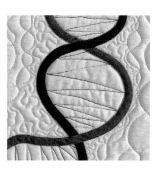

Many historic appliqué quilts, especially the classic Baltimore Album quilts, include baskets made of woven bias strips. The process fascinates me even though baskets don't really suit my quilting style, so for this table topper, I adapted the basic weaving idea to a more abstract design inspired by the twisted shape of DNA molecules. This project is a good intro to appliquéing bias strips, as there's no pattern to follow: just bend the curves as you go. If you're used to sewing with fabrics you *don't* want to stretch on the bias, it's fun to instead take advantage of the bias to work more fluidly than stable straight grains allow.

choosing fabric

Keeping with the woven theme, I used yarn-dyed, cross-woven fabrics for the bias strips in colors that sparkle against the neutral gray background. The perpendicular warp and weft threads of these fabrics are different colors; your eye blends them together, but they look a little different depending on the viewing angle, so they're especially lively when textured with quilting.

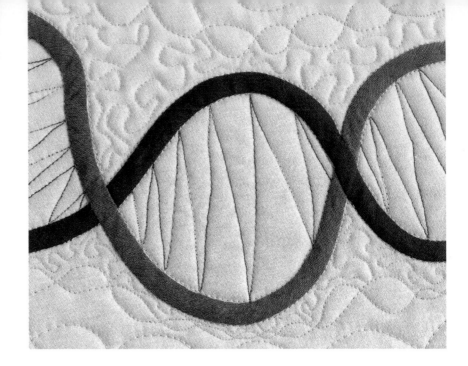

CUT THE FABRIC

1 • From gray background fabric, cut:

▷ 1 Background circle 24½" (62 cm) diameter using the template. Transfer the dotted guide circle to the Background piece.

2 • From each yarn-dyed fabric, cut:

▷ 3 bias strips ¾" (2 cm) wide (or width directed by tape-maker's instructions).

PREPARE THE BIAS STRIPS AND BACKGROUND

3 • Join the same-color bias strips with diagonal seams to make one strip of each fabric about 72" (183 cm) long.

4 • Run each strip through the bias-tape maker to turn the edges under.

5 • Glue-baste one of the bias strips angling across the guide circle, leaving a 12" (30.5 cm) tail. Leaving a 24" (61 cm) tail and angling in the opposite direction, glue-baste the remaining bias strip on top of the first as shown **(fig. 1)**. Gently curve the strips away from the circle and back toward it again, glue-basting as you work. Bring the strips toward each other to meet again near the guide circle, overlapping the strips opposite to the way they overlapped at the start. Continue gluing the strips to the Background, curving in and out and alternating the overlap at each intersection, about two-thirds of the way around the circle. The organic look of the helixes comes from varying the depth of the curves and the shape of the spaces enclosed by the strips, so don't worry about making them too consistent. For reference, the sample has a total of 10 loops, averaging 4½" (11.5 cm)

Improvisational Prepared-Edge Appliqué

The sewing process used with starch-turned appliqué doesn't lend itself easily to improvisational work—once the edges are turned, that's the shape you're going to sew. But that doesn't mean the technique has no improvisational potential. There's no limit to the possible line drawings you could make on a quilt top with bias strips by layering, bending, and weaving them over each other. You could starch-turn a bunch of circles, then glue them up at random, like bubbles bouncing around the block. Or just cut templates freehand from doubled freezer paper without drawing a pattern first—you could make a turned-edge version of the Cobblestones Quilt (page 48) from the previous chapter or the All Seasons Pillows (page 126) from the next one this way. Or become a textile-art Matisse and chop freezer paper into random shapes to make templates for entirely new designs.

variations

Intertwined, free-form bias strips could be placed in a straight line rather than a circle—perhaps multiple rows of helix loops stacked up to make a quilt—or you could braid together three or more strips. When I looked at a photo of the finished table topper, the five bulges of each color strip seemed to form an abstract human figure with a head, two arms, and two legs—you could "draw" all kinds of shapes using bias-strip outlines.

long—the number of loops needs to be even for the ends of the strips to match up.

6 • As you approach the starting point again, plan your curves so the ends of the strips will meet smoothly (if necessary, dissolve the basting glue of previous curves with a little water and reposition them). Using the tails from the start of each bias strip, position the strips so their ends meet under an intersection of the second color to hide the join. When you're satisfied with the strip placement, cut the excess from each end (making sure the cut will be hidden) and securely glue-baste the cut ends under the overlapping strip **(fig. 2)**.

APPLIQUÉ THE STRIPS

7 • Blindstitch the folded edges of the bias strips to the Background using fine matching thread. At intersections, sew the uppermost strip to the strip below; for the lower strip, pass the thread under the intersection to continue sewing beyond it, or end the thread where the strip is covered.

QUILT AND FINISH

To give the inside of the loops of bias strips a little more punch, I free-motion quilted zigzags using variegated thread with shades related to the bias-strip colors. I filled the background with circles of curved, crisscrossing lines, like smaller versions of the bias loops, and filled smaller areas with meandering. I also outlined the bias loops with quilting to help define them.

8 • Trim the backing fabric to 27" (68.5 cm) square. Layer the backing right side up on the batting square. Place the appliquéd top right sides together with the backing and baste the layers together. Using the cut edge of the Background circle as a guide, sew the layers together with a ¼" (6 mm) seam allowance, leaving an opening of about 9" (23 cm) for turning. Trim the excess batting and backing flush with the edge of the

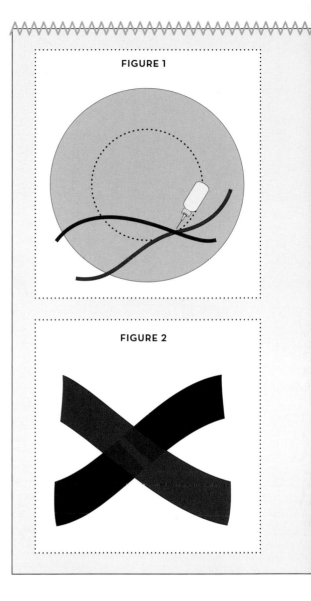

FIGURE 1

FIGURE 2

Background circle, then cut notches into the seam allowance every 1" to 2" (2.5 to 5 cm), cutting almost to the stitching line but being careful not to cut through it. Turn the topper right side out, press the seam allowances in along the opening, and topstitch ⅛" (3 mm) from the outer edge all around the topper, closing the opening. Topstitch around the perimeter again ¼" (6 mm) inside the previous stitching.

9 • Quilt as desired.

NEEDLE-TURN APPLIQUÉ

The needle-turn method of appliqué dispenses with elaborate preparation and uses little more than a needle to turn under seam allowances as you sew. It has an unjust reputation for being challenging—I find it the most enjoyable appliqué method.

why needle-turn appliqué?

Needle-turn appliqué, in which you turn the edges of the appliqués under with your needle tip as you sew them to the background, is the most "traditional" of quiltmakers' appliqué techniques. Regardless of tradition, it's my favorite way to appliqué. The process is streamlined (especially with the use of modern tools such as basting glue), and compared to starch-turned prepared-edge appliqué, the preparation is minimal—for the All Seasons Pillows (page 126) and Garden Allotments Quilt (page 120), I didn't even use templates—which means you can dive right into the sewing. After all the time I spent designing the blocks for the Fruit Market Quilt (page 132), I was itching to sew,

and needle-turn let me get my hands on the fabric quickly to start the fun of seeing the final shapes emerge while turning the seam allowances under. I like the organic quality of defining the edges as I sew, making this method appropriate for a freeform design such as my Eccentric Concentrics Wall Quilt (page 114), which would have been needlessly complicated by figuring out how to do it with templates.

But more than all of that, needle-turn appliqué is just the process I enjoy the most. For me, at least, it's fun and even relaxing. I encourage you to give it a try and see if you feel the same.

✿ tip

Make sure your sharp embroidery scissors are handy—trimming and clipping seam allowances will give them a workout.

tools and supplies

One of the great things about needle-turn appliqué is the short list of specialized tools required.

TOOLS FOR TRANSFERRING PATTERNS

Freezer paper is useful for transferring pattern shapes to fabric. Fine-grit sandpaper placed underneath the fabric keeps it from stretching while being marked.

MARKING TOOLS

Removable marking tools that contrast with your fabric are used for indicating the edges of the appliqué shapes, guiding your stitching and turning of the seam allowance.

BASTING GLUE AND FRAY PREVENTER

Hold appliqués in place with basting glue. For fabrics that tend to fray or seam allowances that are on the tiny side, a dab of fray preventer (such as Fray Check) can make things easier.

Aside from scissors, a needle, and thread, that's really all you need!

Needle-Turn Appliqué at a Glance

TOOLBOX
- Freezer paper
- Sandpaper (optional)
- Removable marking tools
- Basting glue
- Fray preventer (optional)
- Scissors
- Needles
- Thread

PATTERNS AND TEMPLATES
- Use non-reversed pattern to trace shapes onto the appliqué fabric (optionally via freezer paper).
- Use non-reversed pattern to arrange shapes on background.
- Tracings on fabric have no seam allowances; add seam allowances when cutting fabric.

NEEDLES AND THREAD

My first choice for needle-turn appliqué is fine size 100 silk thread, such as that made by YLI. The thread is strong but so fine that it sinks in between the woven fibers of the fabric and disappears. As a result, you can get away with only dark and light neutral colors to start with, though a color that nearly matches the appliqué is best. I like a no. 11 sharps needle with this thread. The thread and purpose-made appliqué needles are available in many quilt shops, and though the spools are a bit pricey, they last a long time.

Fine cotton threads, size 60, are good alternatives if silk thread is difficult to find or prohibitively expensive. They require a little extra care to keep hidden, but some quilters prefer that the thread fiber matches that of the fabric. Though polyester remains a dirty word in the quilting community, some manufacturers have introduced lightweight next-generation threads that have started to catch on with some appliqué enthusiasts. These threads, such as WonderFil's size 100 Invisafil thread, dispense with the negative qualities associated with poor-quality polyester sewing thread and behave much like silk thread, but at a more economical price.

Tools and supplies for needle-turn appliqué:
❶ Handsewing needles
❷ Silk thread ❸ ❹ ❺
Fine cotton threads ❻ ❼
Marking tools ❽ Basting glue ❾ Freezer-paper template on right side of fabric.

Fine silk thread hides ▶ appliqué stitches, letting the Fruit Market Quilt's (page 132) shapes, fabrics, and quilting do the talking.

techniques

The following is an overview of putting blocks together for needle-turn appliqué. Some of the motions, such as sweeping the seam allowances under with your needle, may seem awkward at first, but they'll become second nature with practice.

TRANSFERRING DESIGNS BY FREEZER-PAPER TRACING

I use this method when I want the appliqué shapes to be precise copies of the pattern. Note that this is a different technique than the freezer-paper templates used for prepared-edge appliqué (see page 72).

1 • Place a single layer of freezer paper over the pattern, dull side up. Trace the shapes onto the freezer paper with a pencil **(fig. 1)**, leaving a little space between them. If the pattern includes the same shape repeated multiple times, you need to trace it only once. Label the pieces if necessary to avoid confusion.

2 • Cut the traced shapes out of the freezer paper along the drawn lines **(fig. 2)**.

3 • Press the freezer-paper shapes shiny side down onto the right side of the fabric, leaving at least ½" (1.3 cm) between shapes **(fig. 3)**.

4 • Using a contrasting, removable marking tool, lightly trace around the freezer paper to mark its shape on the fabric **(fig. 4)**. It's helpful to place the fabric on fine-grit sandpaper or another slightly rough surface so the marking tool doesn't stretch the fabric; if I don't have sandpaper handy, I use a somewhat worn self-healing cutting mat instead. Peel off the freezer paper and repress it elsewhere on the fabric if multiples of the same shape are needed.

5 • Cut out the shapes traced onto the fabric ¼" (6 mm) outside the lines **(fig. 5)**.

TRANSFERRING DESIGNS BY DIRECT TRACING

This quick-and-dirty technique can stretch the fabric slightly, so I tend to use it when some departure from the exact shapes of the pattern is acceptable.

1 • Place the pattern on a light box or bright window. Place the appliqué fabric right side up over it **(fig. 6)**.

2 • Using a contrasting removable marking tool, lightly trace the pattern shapes onto the fabric, leaving at least ½" (1.3 cm) between shapes. A light touch with the marking tool helps prevent stretching the fabric **(fig. 7)**.

3 • Cut out the shapes traced onto the fabric ¼" (6 mm) outside the lines **(fig. 8)**.

GLUING UP BLOCKS

Basting appliqué pieces to the background is effectively the same process for needle-turn as for prepared-edge appliqué (see page 78), the main difference being that the traced lines of the appliqué shapes should be lined up with the pattern, since the seam allowances haven't been turned under. Dot the basting glue on the wrong side of the appliqués at least ¼" (6 mm) inside of the traced line so it doesn't block the seam allowances you'll be turning under **(fig. 9)**. (If glue does end up in the way, just dampen it and gently peel the fabrics apart.) If pattern pieces are numbered, layer from number 1 upward; where pieces overlap, be sure the lower shape will still extend under the upper shapes when the seam allowances are turned.

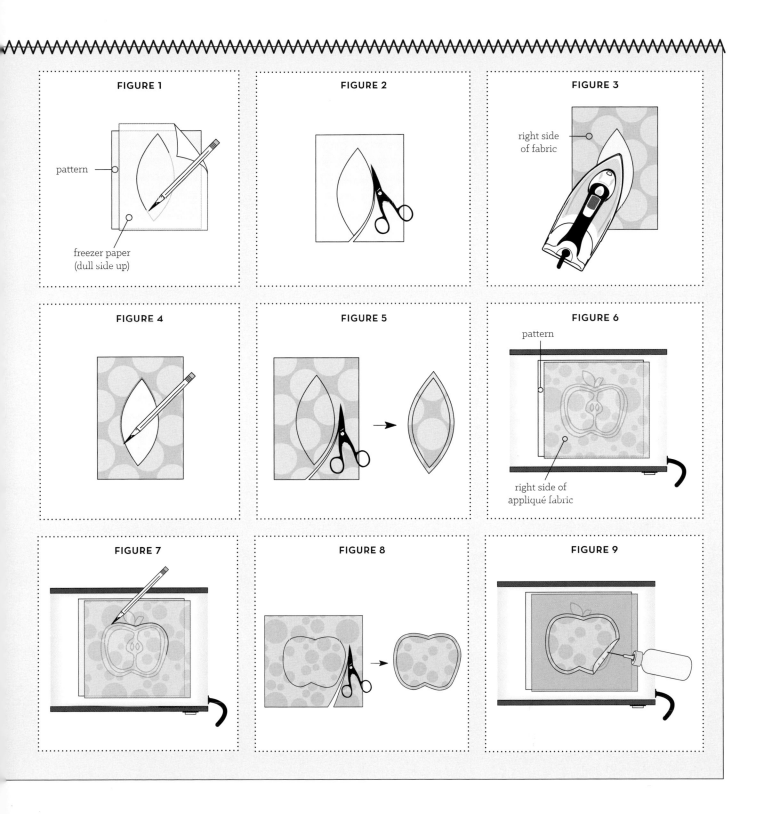

FIGURE 1

pattern

freezer paper
(dull side up)

FIGURE 2

FIGURE 3

right side
of fabric

FIGURE 4

FIGURE 5

FIGURE 6

pattern

right side of
appliqué fabric

FIGURE 7

FIGURE 8

FIGURE 9

SEWING BY HAND WITH A BLINDSTITCH

The basic blindstitch is the same as for prepared-edge appliqué (see page 78), but you'll also be sweeping the raw edge under the fabric as you work your way around the shapes. Start with the lowest layer of fabric—the one closest to the background—and work up to the top layer. Overlapped sections of fabric don't need to be sewn down.

1 • Knot the thread and insert your needle between the appliqué fabric and the background, bringing it up through the line marked on the appliqué shape.

2 • Holding the work with your nondominant hand, use the needle tip to sweep the seam allowance under to the marked line where the needle emerged under the appliqué **(fig. 10)**.

3 • Hold the turned-under fabric in place with the thumb of your nondominant hand. Take the needle through the background fabric immediately next to where it emerged from the appliqué and bring it back through the background and the folded edge of the appliqué about 1/16" (2 mm) from the previous stitch **(fig. 11)**. Try to keep slightly under the fold to help hide the stitches.

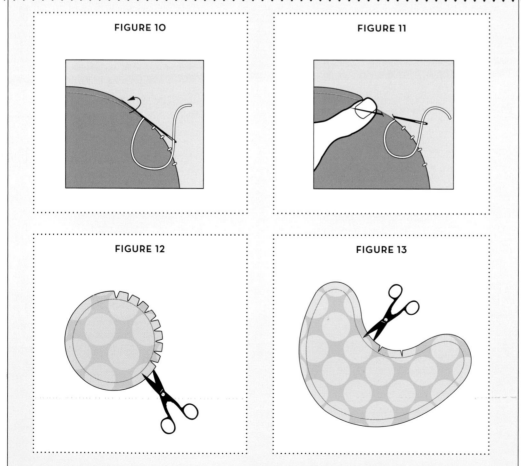

FIGURE 10

FIGURE 11

FIGURE 12

FIGURE 13

Needle-turn appliqué ▶
is perfectly suited to
the organic curves
of the Eccentric
Concentrics Wall
Quilt (page 114).

4 • Sweep ½" (1.3 cm) or so of seam allowance ahead of your stitching under the appliqué, up to the marked line, and hold it with your thumb. Continue sewing as described in Step 3, progressively sweeping the seam allowance under as you move around the shape.

5 • When finished, knot the thread on the back of the work.

Dealing with Outside Curves

I rarely feel the need to clip convex curves, but if the seam allowance seems too bulky under the appliqué or your curves aren't smooth, clip notches out of the seam allowance periodically, making sure the clipping stops a thread or two before the marked line **(fig. 12)**.

Dealing with Inside Curves

Concave curves pull the turned-under seam allowance, so make straight clips into the seam allowance to ease it around inner curves, making sure the clipping stops a thread or two before the marked line **(fig. 13)**. One clip near the center of a fairly short curve may be enough; make periodic clips along longer curved areas, as frequently as needed to sew a smooth curve.

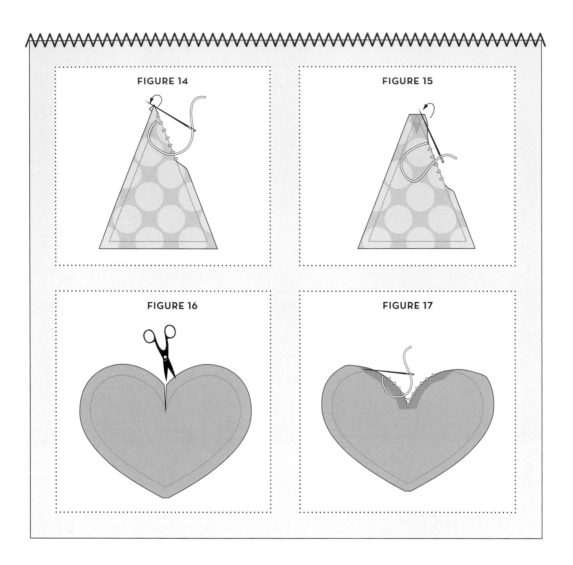

With lots of inside ▶ corners between petals, the Garden Allotments Quilt (page 120) is great for building your needle-turn skills.

FIGURE 14

FIGURE 15

FIGURE 16

FIGURE 17

Dealing with Outside Points

Sew up to the tip along the first side, which will leave a dog-ear extending from the other side of the point. Secure the tip of the point with a stitch, then tuck the dog-ear under with your needle before turning the seam allowance under and sewing down the second side **(fig. 14)**. Or turn under the tip of the point before you've sewn the first side, then turn under the seam allowances along each side while sewing **(fig. 15)**.

Dealing with Inside Corners

This is the most challenging area to sew simply because there isn't any seam allowance at a sharp corner: it folds under both sides of the corner, spreading away from the point itself. At the corner, clip the seam allowance right up to the drawn line **(fig. 16)**. After turning the seam allowance under along the first side, take an extra stitch or two to secure the corner itself; since there's little or no seam allowance at this exact point, you'll need to overcast a couple threads of the fabric. Then continue needle-turning the next side **(fig. 17)**.

ECCENTRIC CONCENTRICS WALL QUILT

APPLIQUÉ TECHNIQUE
Needle-turn reverse appliqué

FINISHED SIZE
35" × 40" (89 × 101.5 cm)

MATERIALS
- ○ 1⅛ yd (103 cm) each of 5 solid and/or print fabrics (less fabric may be used for the uppermost layers; see Step 6)

- ○ 1⅓ yd (122 cm) backing fabric

- ○ ⅜ yd (34.5 cm) binding fabric

- ○ 43" × 48" (109 × 122 cm) batting

TOOLS
- ○ Removable marking tool

- ○ Safety pins

- ○ Toolbox for needle-turn appliqué (page 105)

- ○ Gridded Pattern (page 117)

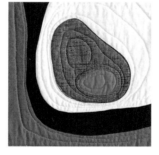

Appliqué is an inherently dimensional technique. Sure, cotton fabrics are nearly flat, but the slight thickness of appliqué shapes does build up into a sort of bas-relief on the background surface. Reverse appliqué turns this effect on its head: the background fabric is cut away and sewn to the layer beneath, so instead of building up, the layers go deeper into the quilt from the surface. You could make Eccentric Concentrics with typical non-reverse appliqué, building the blobby shapes up on each other, but I think the design pulls you in more when the layers are instead excavated one by one.

choosing fabric

Printed and solid fabrics aren't just two sides of the same coin: color is printed onto print fabrics, while solids are typically colored with dyes. That's why solids are the same color on the front and back, whereas prints have a definite right and wrong side. The coloring processes have different properties, as I discovered while choosing fabric for this quilt: none of the dyed solid fabrics I could find could compete with the vibrancy of the hot-pink print I eventually used. The print, though, was a happy addition to the solid fabrics. Remember that limiting yourself to a particular family of fabrics can do your quilt a disservice.

PREPARE THE FABRIC

1 • Designate each fabric with a letter, designating A as the uppermost fabric and E as the lowermost fabric. For example, the sample used the following fabrics:

A	rose pink solid
B	red-pink solid
C	white solid
D	hot pink print
E	orange solid

2 • Press fabric A into quarters and open again. With a removable marking tool, mark a line 2½" (6.5 cm) to each side of the vertical crease and mark another line directly on the horizontal center crease. Starting from these lines, mark a grid of lines 5" (12.5 cm) apart with a removable marking tool. Referring to the Gridded Pattern (page 117), enlarge the A

lines from each grid square from the pattern into the corresponding square on fabric A. Extend design lines to the edges of the fabric if the design stops before the fabric edge.

3 • Place fabric A over fabric B, right sides up and selvedges and raw edges aligned. (If the fabrics weren't cut exactly the same size, the raw edges may not line up perfectly. As long as the overall width of the stacked fabrics is at least 35" [89 cm], you're fine.) Baste the fabrics together with safety pins at least ½" (1.3 cm) beyond the design lines in the sections that won't be cut away.

4 • Cut away the portions of fabric A enclosed by the design lines, leaving about ¼" (6 mm) seam allowance to turn under and making sure **not** to cut into fabric B below. Glue-baste the layers together ¼" (6 mm) past the design lines **(fig. 1)**.

APPLIQUÉ THE SHAPES

5 • Sew the cut edges of fabric A to fabric B using the needle-turn method (page 110). When the appliqué for fabric A is complete, trim away the underlayer of fabric B where it doesn't show through to the front, leaving at least ¼" (6 mm) seam allowance **(fig. 2)**. Trimming will prevent you from having to quilt through up to 5 layers of fabric,

✿ tip

The prep and assembly are a little different for reverse appliqué, but the instructions will guide you through it. The sewing process with reverse appliqué is exactly the same as for regular needle-turn, so it's really not as foreign as you might imagine.

Enlarging the Pattern

If you're confident, it's easiest to just sketch the design freehand onto the fabric, either referring to my pattern or coming up with one entirely your own. But if you do want to rely on my pattern, there are a few alternative enlargement methods to consider. If you have access to an opaque projector, place it over the Gridded Pattern (page 117) and project the enlargement onto fabric hung on a design wall—that's what I did. Or enlarge the Gridded Pattern by 600% on a photocopier and transfer it to the fabric with washable dressmaker's carbon paper. Any of these methods may cause some distortion, but since the design is completely abstract, these variations only make your quilt more unique.

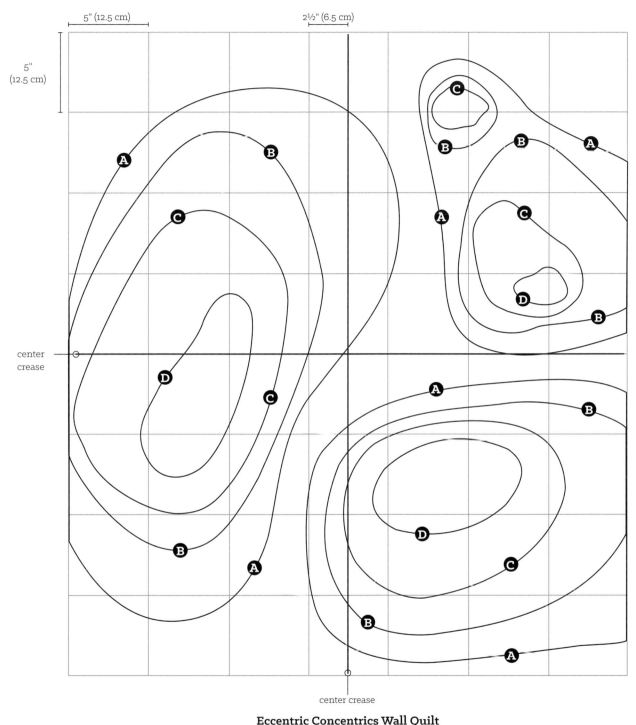

5" (12.5 cm)

2½" (6.5 cm)

5" (12.5 cm)

center crease

center crease

Eccentric Concentrics Wall Quilt
Gridded Pattern
1 grid square = 5" (12.5 cm)
Enlarge by 600% for full-size pattern.

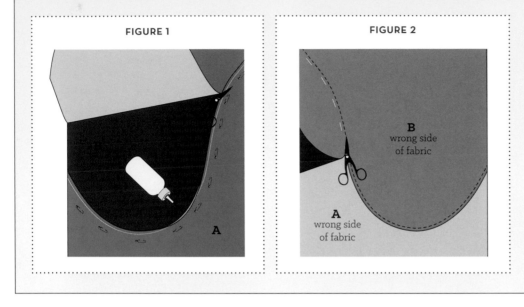

| FIGURE 1 | FIGURE 2 |

In Figure 2:
B wrong side of fabric
A wrong side of fabric

and it also minimizes show-through of darker fabrics. Save the cut-away fabric for another project.

6 • Transfer the corresponding design lines to fabric B as you did for fabric A, extending the grid lines over fabric B if necessary. Place the previously appliquéd fabrics over fabric C, baste with safety pins, carefully cut out the enclosed portions of fabric B, and glue-baste the cut edges. Appliqué the cut edges of fabric B as before, then cut away excess fabric C from the back. Continue following this sequence to add and appliqué subsequent layers of fabric until you've completed the fifth layer. The portions of fabrics D and E that show in the finished quilt top are significantly smaller than the previous fabrics, so you may be able to get away with only ½ yard (45.5 cm) of each—just make sure the basted fabric completely covers the portion that will be cut away from the previous fabric and be

careful that any smaller cuts of fabric are securely basted to the appliquéd sections so the finished top is flat.

QUILT AND FINISH

My quilting pattern was inspired by the contour lines on a topographical map, flowing around the appliqué shapes to unify them. I also made sure to quilt near the edges of each appliquéd shape to reinforce the "seam" made by the appliqué stitching, since the fabric is cut away underneath.

7 • Baste the backing, batting, and quilt top together. Quilt as desired. Trim the quilt sandwich to 35" × 40" (89 × 101.5 cm), squaring the edges as you go.

8 • From binding fabric, cut 4 strips 2" (5 cm) × width of fabric. Join the binding strips with diagonal seams and press in half wrong sides together. Bind the quilt.

variations

Try adding a layer or two of "regular"— that is, not reverse—appliqué on the uppermost layer for more dimension. Or take the topographical contour concept further and use a map of your favorite hills and valleys to design your own reverse-appliqué quilt. With several patterned fabrics, a quilt made with this technique could look like layers of wallpaper being peeled away in an old house—maybe a Victorian print for the innermost layer, moving through period styles such as Art Deco, wild sixties florals, and pop geometrics.

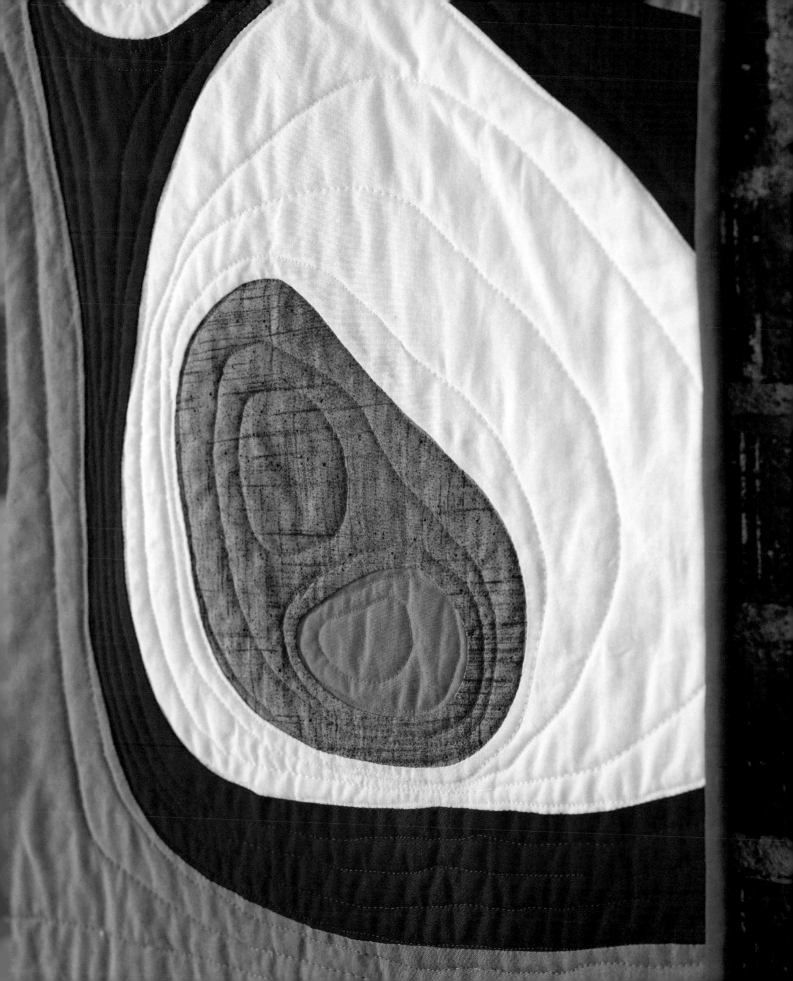

GARDEN ALLOTMENTS QUILT

APPLIQUÉ TECHNIQUES
Needle-turn appliqué with broderie perse

FINISHED SIZE
47" × 56" (119.5 × 142 cm)

MATERIALS
○ 1½ yd (137 cm) total assorted floral prints for blocks, plus additional yardage for appliqués (amount depends on scale, repeat, and design of fabric)

○ 1⅝ yd (149 cm) cream solid fabric for sashing

○ 3⅛ yd (2.86 m) backing fabric

○ ½ yd (45.5 cm) binding fabric

○ 55" × 64" (139.5 × 162.5 cm) batting

TOOLS
○ Toolbox for needle-turn appliqué (page 105)

Though the first fabrics I bought for this quilt came from a fantastic vintage fabric shop in Berlin, it was English garden styles that inspired the design. I spent part of my childhood in the English countryside, where cottage gardens overflow with a hodgepodge of plantings, then as a young adult in London, I saw allotments where city dwellers rent tiny patches of land to grow vegetables and flowers. The quilt combines the structure of the urban allotments with the planned chaos of the cottage garden to showcase large-scale prints that (quite literally) burst from the seams.

choosing fabric

"What line did you use?" is a frequent question when quilters see this quilt. But the fabrics aren't from a single line—in fact, they're all from different lines, made by different manufacturers, and the two vintage fabrics I included were made at least thirty years before the more contemporary prints. No modern-day fabric line would include this many florals in this similar a scale—a large-scale focus print would more likely be combined with a coordinating stripe, geometric, dot, and maybe a tiny floral. In collecting fabrics for this quilt, I looked for a type: exuberant florals, fairly large scale, well-defined edges, with red, black, gold, and white predominating. Orange ties in the fabrics that have green instead of gold—not the sort of left-field coloring you'd find in a designer fabric line, but more lively for it.

CUT THE FABRIC

1 • From floral prints, cut:

> ▷ 30 Block squares, 7½" × 7½" (19 × 19 cm).

2 • From cream solid fabric, cut:

> ▷ 2 Vertical Borders 52½" × 2½" (133.5 × 6.5 cm)

> ▷ 2 Horizontal Borders 47½" × 2½" (120.5 × 6.5 cm)

> ▷ 5 Horizontal Sashings 43½" × 2½" (110.5 × 6.5 cm)

> ▷ 24 Vertical Sashings 2½" × 7½" (6.5 × 19 cm).

3 • From remaining floral prints, cut flower motifs about ¼" (6 mm) outside their outer edges to use for broderie perse. The best flowers to cut are isolated images, not obscured by overlapping motifs, but you can

Broderie Perse

If you've been holding on to big floral prints because they're either too special to cut into or too big in scale to be easily used (or both!), broderie perse shows off such fabrics spectacularly. Defined as appliqué using the motifs printed on the fabric, broderie perse was originally developed as a way to get more impact from small bits of precious, exotic printed chintz imported to Western Europe from India by cutting sections from the fabric and appliquéing them to a larger, plainer background. Often these fabrics featured lavish floral designs, so the spirit of the Garden Allotments Quilt isn't that far from that of an eighteenth-century broderie perse quilt, even though the look is quite different.

I've used needle-turn appliqué to sew the broderie perse here, but it lends itself to other techniques, too. Many quilters like to fuse the cut motifs and sew around them with a hand or machine blanket stitch (of course, you wouldn't add a seam allowance when cutting the motifs in this case), or you might try machine sewing raw-edge shapes with monofilament thread. And while I've said I don't often topstitch raw edges, doing so makes for a casual look that can perfectly suit the collage-like approach of broderie perse.

Think of broderie perse as the ultimate fussy cutting. Florals, of course, are only the tip of the iceberg—any well-defined image could be cut from a print and appliquéd. It doesn't have to be an all-or-nothing technique, either: a single butterfly or other motif could be added to a piece of otherwise conventional appliqué as a special touch. (If you look closely, you might be able to see the one butterfly I mixed in with the flowers in Garden Allotments.)

use overlapped groups of flowers and foliage as a single unit. Cut as many or as few flowers as you like; my sample uses about 25 large- to medium-size flowers and a handful of small leaves. You don't have to cut them all now; feel free to come back and cut more as you lay your quilt out.

ASSEMBLE QUILT SECTIONS

The effect of this quilt comes from the broderie perse overlapping the piecing seams, so you won't be working on isolated block backgrounds. To keep the amount of fabric in your hands manageable, piece the quilt top in 3 sections before working the majority

variations

The vast array of floral fabrics available means you can make a version of this quilt with a totally different feel—soft and cottagey, Jacobean, Asian, or any other style that speaks to you or a potential gift recipient. The simple piecing also makes it easy to alter the size of the quilt: try making a table runner with just one or two rows of blocks. Of course, there's no reason you have to stick to florals. What else might be interesting spilling out of blocks? Zoo animals escaping the blocks that pen them in? Even bold geometric prints breaking out of the piecing structure could be an interesting deconstruction of the conventional quilt framework.

of the appliqué. Press all seam allowances toward the floral Blocks.

4 • Arrange the floral Blocks in 6 rows of 5 blocks each. Piece each row together with a Vertical Sashing strip between each pair of Blocks. Sew a Horizontal Sashing strip along the bottom of every row except Row 6 (the

final row) Sew the rows together in groups of 2: Rows 1 and 2, Rows 3 and 4, and Rows 5 and 6. (See Assembly Diagram, page 125.)

5 • On a design wall or other flat work surface, arrange the broderie perse flowers on each of the pieced sections, overlapping the seams as shown in the sample. Try to create an overall balance of flowers spilling out of the blocks. (You can place some flowers over the raw edges between sections to get a sense of the overall design, but you won't be able to appliqué them down until after the sections have been pieced together; pin them out of the way of the seams or take a digital photo for reference.) Glue-baste the broderie perse flowers in place at least ¼" (6 mm) inside the outer edge of the floral motifs.

6 • Working with each section separately, needle-turn appliqué the broderie perse flowers in place. If your flowers have strongly defined outlines printed around their edges, decide whether to turn these outlines under completely or retain them; match your thread to the color of the flower that will show at the finished edge (see The Skinny on Thin Petals at right).

JOIN THE SECTIONS

7 • Pin and sew the upper and middle quilt sections together along their adjacent edge, and press. If you planned any of your broderie perse flowers to be placed over this seam, appliqué them now. Then sew the lower section on and appliqué any flowers that overlap the seam.

8 • Pin and sew a Vertical Border strip to each quilt top long edge and press. Sew a Horizontal Border strip to each quilt top short edge and press. Appliqué any flowers that overlap the border seams.

QUILT AND FINISH

I quilted the sashing and borders with a meander variation to help them recede into the background. To bring some of the dimension of the appliquéd flowers to the prints they spill out of, I quilted the outlines of the larger flowers in each block as well as quilting around the appliqués. I also quilted around flower centers or other internal

The Skinny on Thin Petals

The most difficult flower motifs to appliqué with this technique are those with deep areas of background color between long petals—when there's only ⅛" (3 mm) separating two petals, there just isn't enough fabric to turn under on both sides of your cut. Aside from skipping these motifs entirely, you have a few choices for dealing with them:

- **Keep the background.** If the background color of the floral fabric is relatively close to the sashing, or if you can place the area in question on the floral Block, it won't be too noticeable if you leave the section between petals intact rather than splitting into two micro seam allowances.
- **Widen the interpetal space.** Sweep some of each petal's edge under, sacrificing a little of the petal width to give enough fabric to turn.
- **Call in the fray preventer.** A touch of your favorite fray-stopping liquid can give the tiny seam allowances enough security to turn.

I used a combination of these approaches on a case-by-case basis. And after sweating over a few tricky daisies, I decided to limit my use of flowers to those without skinny channels—they're still there in the print Blocks, but who says they have to be the ones to spill out?

outlines to stabilize the larger flowers. For smaller-scale prints, I just quilted the background sections without following the foreground motifs too slavishly.

9 • Cut the backing fabric into 2 equal lengths. Sew these sections together with a horizontal seam to make a backing at least 55" × 64" (139.5 × 162.5 cm).

10 • Baste the backing, batting, and quilt top together. Quilt as desired. Trim the excess batting and backing and square the edges of the quilt when finished.

11 • From binding fabric, cut 6 strips 2" (5 cm) × width of fabric. Join the binding strips with diagonal seams and press in half wrong sides together. Bind the quilt.

47½" × 2½" (120.5 × 6.5 cm)

7½" × 7½" (19 × 19 cm)

2½" × 7½" (6.5 × 19 cm)

Row 1

43½" × 2½" (110.5 × 6.5 cm)

Row 2

52½" × 2½" (133.5 × 6.5 cm)

Row 3

Row 4

Row 5

Row 6

Assembly Diagram

ALL SEASONS PILLOWS

APPLIQUÉ TECHNIQUE
Improvisational needle-turn appliqué

FINISHED SIZE
18" × 18" (45.5 × 45.5 cm)

MATERIALS (FOR 1 PILLOW)
- ⅜ yd (34.5 cm) white solid fabric for background

- 9 scraps assorted solids and prints in related colors for appliqués, each about 5" × 5" (12.5 × 12.5 cm)

- ⅝ yd (57 cm) backing fabric

- ½ yd (45.5 cm) solid fabric for piping

- 19" × 19" (48.5 × 48.5 cm) muslin

- 19" × 19" (48.5 × 48.5 cm) batting

- 2¼ yd (2 m) piping cord, ¼" (6 mm) diameter

- Black pearl cotton, size 8 and size 12

- 18" (45.5 cm) square pillow form

Continued on next page…▼

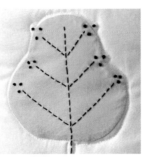

Give these pillows a try if you want to get the feel of needle-turn without worrying about following a line exactly—the pillows are designed to encourage freeform variation. In fact, you can skip the templates completely if you like—I cut the appliqués for each pillow completely freehand and sewed them down freehand, too. (Templates are provided, though, if you want some guidance.) The embroidery was also sewn with very few markings for a casual, organic effect, like hand-drawn pen-and-ink lines against a splotch of colored paint. Why should your work look like it was sewn by a robot? If you're sewing by hand, let it show!

. . . continued from previous page.

TOOLS

○ 5" (12.5 cm) hand-embroidery hoop

○ Thick towel

○ Zipper foot

○ Tree templates (pattern insert C)

○ Toolbox for needle-turn appliqué (page 105)

choosing fabric

Prints are used very sparingly in these pillows, so each one was chosen carefully. I didn't want them to upstage the embroidery, so I focused on subtle, low-contrast prints. But I also wanted them to be appropriate to the theme: the prints I chose all feature leaves or flowers, perfectly at home in a tree. They're not literal depictions of what flowers or leaves of specific trees would look like, but they extend the design intent of the pillow into the fabric for a more holistic design.

CUT THE FABRIC

1 • From white background fabric, cut:

▷ 9 Background squares, 6½" × 6½" (16.5 × 16.5 cm).

2 • Using the templates or cutting freehand (see Almost Freehand, opposite), cut 9 tree shapes, 1 of each shape (or as desired). The template shapes include seam allowances, so cut the pieces directly on the solid lines.

PREPARE AND APPLIQUÉ THE BLOCKS

3 • Glue-baste each tree shape in the center of a Background square. (Since the embroidered trunks will extend below the tree shape, you may want to place some trees slightly higher than center.)

4 • Sew the edges of the tree shapes to the Backgrounds using a blindstitch (page 110), sweeping under about ¼" (6 mm) of the raw edge. For the organic look of the tree shapes, your seam allowance doesn't need to be precise.

EMBROIDER THE BRANCH DETAILS

5 • Referring to the Assembly and Embroidery Diagrams (page 131) or creating your own designs, embroider the branches and trunk of each tree, working with the block in an embroidery hoop. (See page 24 for more on embroidery.) For stitches with a single thickness of thread (such as backstitch, detached chain, and running stitch), I used size 8 pearl cotton. For stitches with more thread buildup (mainly stem stitch), I used finer size 12 pearl cotton to keep the overall lines of stitching a comparable visual weight. I marked guidelines only for the more complex loopy and curlicue designs; everything else was stitched freehand to reinforce the organic appliqué.

ASSEMBLE THE PILLOW FRONT

6 • Arrange the embroidered blocks in 3 rows of 3 blocks each on a design wall or other work surface, varying colors, values, and embroidery patterns.

7 • When you're satisfied with the layout, sew the blocks in each row together. Press the seam allowances to one side, alternating direction between rows.

8 • Pin and sew the rows together. Press the seam allowances to one side. With the assembled pillow front right side down on a thickly folded towel (to avoid flattening the embroidery), press the entire pillow front.

variations

If you already have plenty of pillows, you could piece these tree blocks into a band for embellishing towels or even lightweight curtains. And though I hope I've convinced you of how fun appliqué is by this point, you could skip it altogether and use an embroidery outline instead of the fabric tree shapes—or try to fill in the tree shapes solidly with a filling stitch, and you'll see why appliqué really isn't all that time-consuming compared to some alternatives!

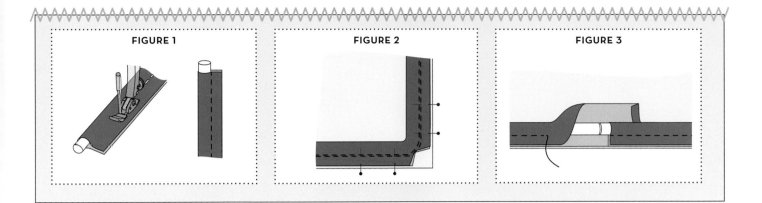

FIGURE 1 | **FIGURE 2** | **FIGURE 3**

9 • Baste the muslin, batting, and pillow front together. Quilt as desired (I stitched in the ditch and quilted another square ¼" [6 mm] inside the final block seams, then I free-motion outlined each tree shape for extra dimension). Trim the batting and muslin ¼" (6 mm) beyond the outer edges of the pillow front to allow a wider seam allowance for attaching piping.

Almost Freehand

I encourage you to try cutting out the trees freehand, but if you can't bear the thought of appliquéing without a template, the templates can be used. The sewing line you'd typically use for needle-turn appliqué is shown as a dashed line but these templates also include a solid cutting line—try cutting your shapes out on the cutting line and turning under the seam allowances without a sewing line to follow. You'll know the pieces will end up the right size overall, but you'll still have some of the individual character of sewing freehand.

Behind the Scenes

Since the wrong side of your blocks will be hidden when the pillow cover is assembled and quilted, small knots on the back of the work aren't a problem. Embroiderers' guilds would revoke my stitching permit for saying so—and certainly go ahead and hide your thread ends properly if you like!—but this isn't a case where the back will ever be visible, even if someone turns the pillow cover inside out. That said, I do recommend avoiding carrying the thread across the back from place to place, as it may show through the fabric, especially the white fabric. (This is hard to avoid with some stitches, though, like the seeded fly stitches—just try to keep the floats behind the appliquéd shape so there's an extra layer of fabric to conceal them.)

MAKE AND INSERT THE PIPING

10 • From piping fabric, cut 4 bias strips 1¾" (4.5 cm) wide. Join the bias piping strips with diagonal seams. Press the seam allowances open and trim off the dog-ears.

11 • Fold the bias strip around the piping cord, wrong sides together, matching up the long raw edges. Machine-baste along the length of the piping, using a zipper foot to get the needle close to the piping cord **(fig. 1)**.

12 • Leaving a tail of at least 6" (15 cm), pin the piping around the perimeter of the pillow front, aligning the raw edges. Clip into the piping seam allowance to ease it around the corners **(fig. 2)**. Machine-baste the piping to the quilted pillow front with a zipper foot, leaving a loose, overlapping tail of piping at each end. Undo the basting for about 3" (7.5 cm) at one end of the piping, then turn back the fabric to expose the cord. Trim the cord and the piping at the other end to butt against each other, making sure the turned-back fabric will extend at least 1" (2.5 cm) past the join. Finger-press ½" (1.3 mm) under at the end of the turned-back fabric, then rewrap it around the ends of the piping and glue-baste in place **(fig. 3)**. Machine-baste to secure the ends.

ASSEMBLE THE PILLOW

13 • From backing fabric, cut 2 rectangles 13" × 19" (33 × 48.5 cm). Press ½" (1.3 cm) to

the wrong side along one long edge of each Backing rectangle, then press under another ½" (1.3 cm). Topstitch near the fold to hem each Backing rectangle.

14 • Pin a Backing rectangle right sides together with the pillow front, raw edges aligned. Pin the remaining Backing rectangle on top, raw edges aligned with the remaining raw edges of the pillow front so the hemmed sections overlap in the middle.

15 • Using a zipper foot, sew close to the piping cord all the way around the pillow. Clip the corners carefully, then turn the pillow cover right side out through the hemmed opening. Push out the corners gently and press the edges. Insert the pillow form through the back opening.

Improvisational Needle-Turn Appliqué

One of my very first experiments in needle-turning without a pattern involved cutting printed letters out of fabrics to sew into a sort of fabric ransom note—just to spell out a phrase rather than actually demand a ransom, of course. Templates would have got in the way here, since the letters were all different sizes and it didn't matter exactly what shape they ended up.

The fluidity of needle-turn is something I embrace in a lot of my appliqué, even if I do trace the shapes onto the fabric first. In fact, while All Seasons is the only place in this chapter where I cut the shapes completely freehand, there's a little improvisation in every project in the chapter. Eccentric Concentrics is based only loosely on a pattern, and the flower shapes in Garden Allotments were determined by what was printed on the fabric. For Fruit Market, I skipped the precise freezer-paper transfer and instead traced shapes onto the fabric over a light box, so a little stretching here and there resulted in slight deviations from the pattern. Even a precisely traced shape can be a little off if you're turning under just shy of or just past the line—and I think that's perfectly fine! Precision is called for when designs rely on exact geometric shapes for their effect, but treating organic shapes organically can actually enhance the design.

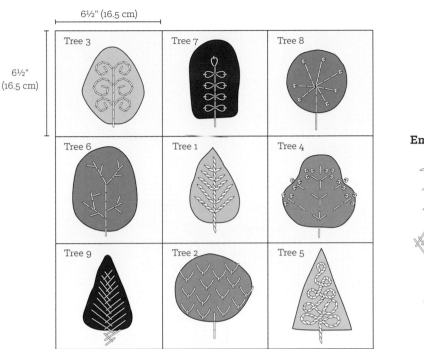

6½" (16.5 cm)

6½" (16.5 cm)

Tree 3　Tree 7　Tree 8

Tree 6　Tree 1　Tree 4

Tree 9　Tree 2　Tree 5

Summer/Fall Assembly and Embroidery Diagram

Embroidery Key

〰️	stem stitch
─│─	backstitch
‑ ‑ ‑	running stitch
〴	leaf stitch
👁	detached chain stitch
ᐯ	fly stitch
•	french knot

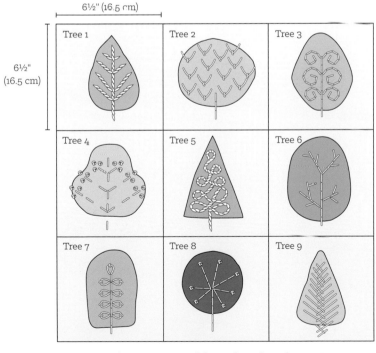

6½" (16.5 cm)

6½" (16.5 cm)

Tree 1　Tree 2　Tree 3

Tree 4　Tree 5　Tree 6

Tree 7　Tree 8　Tree 9

Winter/Spring Assembly and Embroidery Diagram

FRUIT MARKET QUILT

APPLIQUÉ TECHNIQUES
Needle-turn appliqué

FINISHED SIZE
56" × 72" (142 × 183 cm)

MATERIALS
- ○ 2½ yd (2.3 m) total assorted polka dot, stripe, and small floral or fruit prints for appliqué block backgrounds

- ○ 3 yd (2.75 m) total assorted fruit and floral prints for non-appliqué blocks

- ○ 2 yd (1.8 m) total assorted scraps of solid fabrics and stripe and dot prints for fruit appliqués

- ○ Scraps of brown felt or Ultrasuede for small seed appliqués (optional)

- ○ 3⅝ yd (3.32 m) backing fabric

- ○ ½ yd (45.5 cm) binding fabric

- ○ 64" × 80" (162.5 × 203 cm) batting

- ○ Brown pearl cotton, size 5, for embroidering stems

TOOLS
- ○ Fruit patterns (pattern inserts A and B)

- ○ Toolbox for needle-turn appliqué (page 105)

- ○ Light box (optional)

I made this quilt as an homage to the late Jean Ray Laury, whose groundbreaking book *Appliqué Stitchery* was published 1966. She was one of very few quiltmakers at the time who successfully updated the craft of quilting to the visual style of the mid-century era. Some of Laury's most striking motifs—not just in appliqué but in her wood designs and work as an illustrator—are apples, stone fruits, pears, and other fruit, the same imagery found in so many of today's fabric prints. I combined those fabrics with blocks inspired by Laury's fruit designs for a quilt that's an exuberant bounty of juicy produce.

choosing fabric

Like the China Cupboard Wall Quilt (page 60), the fabrics for the plain blocks of Fruit Market share subject matter and a general style. For the appliqués themselves, I brought out the retro feel of the design by restricting most of the fabrics to basic prints that would have been a quilter's staples in Laury's day—polka dots, stripes, and solids. But I took full advantage of today's greatly expanded range of such fabrics, thankfully now available in 100 percent cotton.

CUT THE FABRIC

1 · Refer to the table at right to cut backgrounds for the appliqué blocks and the non-appliqué fruit-print blocks.

2 · Cut and sew fabrics for the pieced appliqués as listed below. Sew each pair of pieces together along a long edge and press the seam allowances open.

▷ For Block F (large pear), cut 1 rectangle at least 4½" × 10½" (11.5 × 26.5 cm) for each half of the pear. I used tan and orange polka dots.

▷ For Block K (large apple), cut 1 rectangle at least 4½" × 7½" (11.5 × 19 cm) for each half of the apple. I used a solid red and a red polka dot.

▷ For Block P (cherries), cut 4 rectangles 1¾" × 6" (4.5 × 15 cm) for halves of the leaves. I used green polka dots and a stripe, angling the stripe to suggest the veins of a leaf. Sew the leaf halves into pairs, one for each leaf.

▷ For Block S (small pear), cut 1 rectangle at least 2½" × 5½" (6.5 × 14 cm) for each half of the pear. I used yellow-green polka dots.

Fabric Cutting Table

SIZE (WIDTH × LENGTH)	CUT FOR APPLIQUÉ BACKGROUNDS	CUT FOR NON-APPLIQUÉ BLOCKS
3" × 9½" (7.5 × 24 cm)	–	1 (Block 25)
7½" × 9½" (19 × 24 cm)	–	3 (Blocks 1, 3, 22)
8½" × 9½" (21.5 × 24 cm)	1 (Block O)	–
11" × 9½" (28 × 24 cm)	5 (Blocks A, D, I, K, L)	1 (Block 17)
14½" × 9½" (37 × 24 cm)	1 (Block C)	2 (Blocks 20, 21)
7½" × 12½" (19 × 31.5 cm)	–	3 (Blocks 4, 7, 15)
11" × 12½" (28 × 31.5 cm)	2 (Blocks F, N)	1 (Block 5)
14½" × 12½" (37 × 31.5 cm)	3 (Blocks E, J, P)	2 (Blocks 19, 24)
7½" × 6½" (19 × 16.5 cm)	6 (Blocks B, G, H, M, Q, S)	6 (Blocks 6, 11, 13, 23, 31, 33)
11" × 6½" (28 × 16.5 cm)	1 (Block R)	4 (Blocks 8, 27, 30, 32)
14½" × 6½" (37 × 16.5 cm)	–	4 (Blocks 10, 28, 29, 34)
4" × 6½" (10 × 16.5 cm)	–	3 (Blocks 9, 12, 14)
7½" × 3½" (19 × 9 cm)	–	1 (Block 2)
11" × 3½" (28 × 9 cm)	–	3 (Blocks 16, 18, 26)

3 · Aligning the seams with the dashed lines on the patterns, transfer the pieced appliqué shapes to the fabrics sewn in the previous step. Transfer the remaining Fruit Appliqué pattern shapes onto your chosen fabrics and cut them out (page 108). (For small seeds, you may prefer to cut felt or Ultrasuede to the finished sizes and use a small overcast stitch to sew them in place.) Note that Block H uses reverse appliqué: cut the enclosed sections away from the main pomegranate shape,

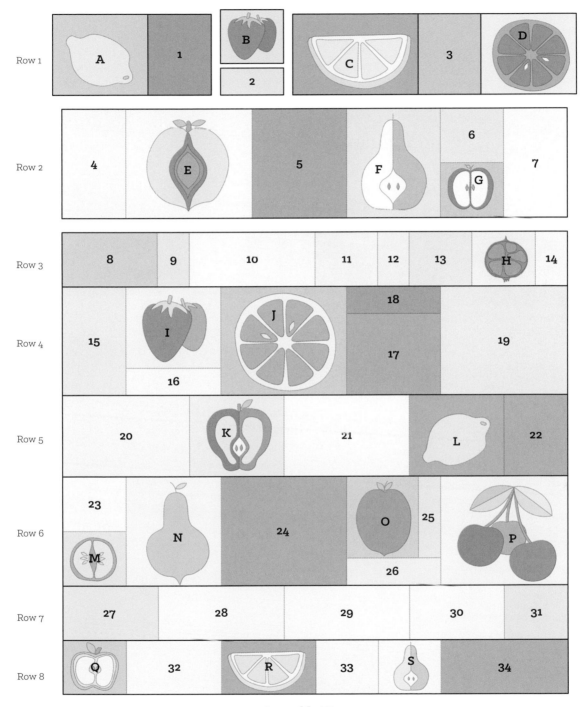

Assembly Diagram

Refer to fabric-cutting table (page 134) for fabric dimensions.

then back it with a piece of fabric cut in the shape of the lighter line on the pattern.

APPLIQUÉ THE BLOCKS

4 • Place a block pattern over a light box or bright window, then center the corresponding background fabric over it. Using a removable marking tool, trace any single stem lines for blocks that don't have appliquéd stems. Glue-baste the appliqué pieces in ascending numerical order. Repeat to prepare each block. For the stems in Block P, make and use ¼" (6 mm) wide bias strips (page 76).

5 • Using the needle-turn method, sew the appliqué pieces down in numerical order as shown on the pattern.

6 • Use pearl cotton to embroider the stems shown as single lines on the block patterns in a stem stitch (page 24).

ASSEMBLE THE QUILT

Press the seam allowances after sewing each seam. Since there are no seams to match in this quilt, I pressed the seam allowances open for a flatter finish, but you can press them to one side if you prefer.

7 • Referring to the Assembly Diagram (page 135), arrange the appliqué and non-appliqué blocks on a design wall or other flat work surface.

8 • Sew any horizontal seams within each row first. For example, sew Block B to Block 2, Block 6 to Block G, etc. In Row 6, sew Block 25 to Block O before sewing Block 26 to the bottom. Return these pieced units to their places on your work surface.

9 • Starting with the top row, pin and sew all the blocks and pieced units in the row together, taking care to keep them in order, then proceed to the next row until you've sewn all 8 rows.

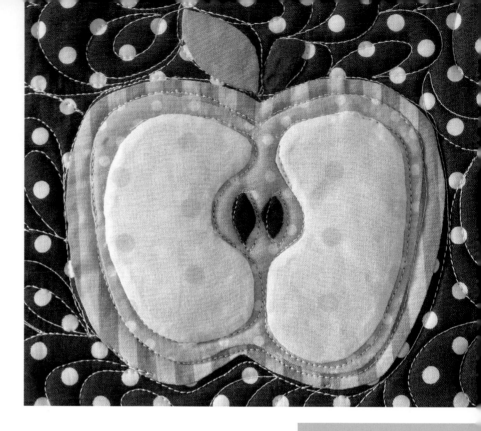

10 • Pin and sew adjacent rows together: sew Rows 1, 2, 3, and 4, then Rows 5, 6, 7, and 8. Pin and sew the 2 halves together.

QUILT AND FINISH

The background of the quilt was quilted on a long-arm machine with a freeform design of feathery concentric loops. Each of the appliqués was outlined, and for the simpler fruits with large open spaces (lemon, lime, plain pear, cherries, and plum), the quilter added a curved bar onto the fruits to suggest the reflection of light hitting the curved surface.

11 • Cut the backing fabric into 2 equal lengths. Sew these sections together with a horizontal seam to make a backing at least 64" × 80" (162.5 × 203 cm).

12 • Baste the backing, batting, and quilt top together. Quilt as desired. Trim the excess batting and backing and square the edges of the quilt.

13 • From binding fabric, cut 7 strips, 2" (5 cm) × width of fabric. Join the binding strips with diagonal seams and press them in half wrong sides together. Bind the quilt.

variations

For a different look, make this quilt using fusible appliqué, with a contrasting thread to define the edges of the fruit shapes. Play around with different block layouts to make the quilt a different size or shape. Or go smaller than a quilt: the fruit appliqués (enlarged or reduced as necessary) would be perfect for embellishing an apron, placemats, or other kitchen items.

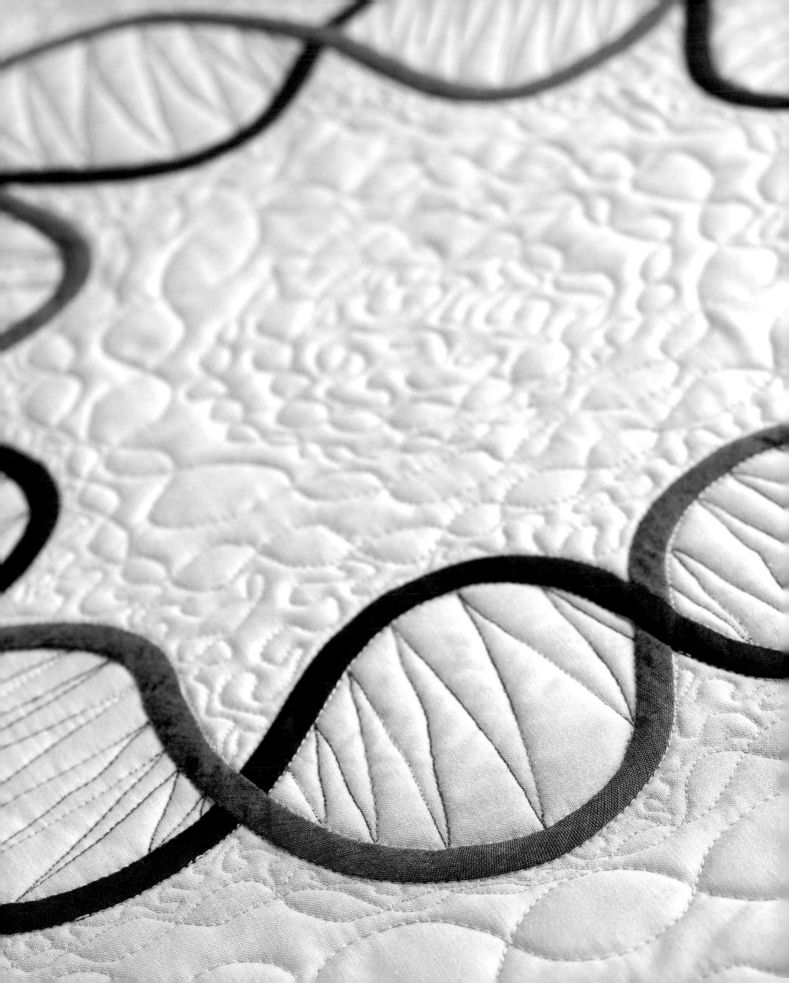

resources

TOOLS AND SUPPLIES

Many supplies are carried by big-box sewing and craft stores, but your local quilt shop is the first port of call for specialty appliqué supplies. If you don't have a well-stocked shop nearby, the Internet puts anything you need only a search away. The contact information below may help you locate a source for some of the specific items mentioned in the book, but note that most of these companies don't sell directly to consumers.

Mettler
amann-mettler.com
Cotton sewing, quilting, and embroidery threads for machine use

Pilot Pen
3855 Regent Blvd.
Jacksonville, FL 32224
(904) 565-7600
pilotpen.us
FriXion heat-removable pens

Roxanne International
distributed by Colonial Needle Company
74 Westmoreland Ave.
White Plains, NY 10606
(800) 963-3353
colonialneedle.com
Needles and basting glue

Therm O Web
770 Glenn Ave.
Wheeling, IL 60090
(800) 323-0799
thermowebonline.com
HeatnBond Lite fusible web

The Warm Company
5529 186th Place SW
Lynnwood, WA 98037
(800) 234-9276
warmcompany.com
Steam-A-Seam 2 double-stick fusible web

WonderFil Specialty Threads
Bay 3, 2915 19th St. NE
Calgary, AB
Canada T2E 7A2
(866) 250-6101
wonderfil.net
InvisaFil 100-weight polyester thread

YLI Corporation
1439 Dave Lyle Blvd.
Rock Hill, SC 29730
(803) 985-3100
ylicorp.com
Silk thread No. 100

BOOKS AND APPS

If you're itching to get more info on a particular technique or want to brush up on quiltmaking basics, these books are great references. I've also included a few out-of-print books that are worth checking out secondhand if, like me, you're inspired by mid-century needlework.

Avery, Virginia. *The Big Book of Appliqué.* New York: Scribners, 1978.
An interesting blend of history, technique, and contemporary (to its period) appliqué that delves into appliqué traditions around the world.

Davis, Boo. *Dare to Be Square Quilting.* New York: Potter Craft, 2010.
Fun projects pieced from rectangles and squares.

Goldsmith, Becky, and Linda Jenkins. *The Best-Ever Appliqué Sampler from Piece O' Cake Designs.* Lafayette, California: C&T Publishing, 2013.
The most recent edition of an extremely detailed appliqué guidebook, focusing on needle-turn techniques.

Hargrave, Harriet. *Mastering Machine Appliqué, 2nd ed.* Lafayette, California: C&T Publishing, 2002.
Invisible-thread, satin-stitched, and blanket-stitched appliqué techniques are covered with lots of technical information.

Howard, Constance. *Inspiration for Embroidery,* 2nd ed. London: B. T. Batsford, 1967.
Embroidery books are often less rigid about appliqué than their quilt-oriented counter-parts; this one is brimming with shapes and ideas for any type of textile design.

Laury, Jean Ray. *Appliqué Stitchery.* New York: Van Nostrand Reinhold, 1966.
A treasure trove of inspiration from a pioneering master quilter.

Mollon, Sandra. *Appliqué* app for iPhone and iPad. Altamont Technologies, 2012.
Video lessons on starch-turned freezer-paper appliqué.

Nickels, Sue, and Pat Holly. *Stitched Raw Edge Appliqué.* Paducah, Kentucky: American Quilter's Society, 2006.
The bible for blanket-stitch, raw-edge machine appliqué, with zigzag stitch as an alternative.

Ringle, Weeks, and Bill Kerr. *The Modern Quilt Workshop.* Gloucester, Massachusetts: Quarry Books, 2005.
A thoughtful introduction to piecing modern quilts, with an education in design principles along the way.

AUTHOR'S WEBSITE
Feed Dog Designs

feeddog.net

acknowledgments

Many thanks are owed to Interweave for making this book what it is. Thanks to Allison Korleski, for immediately grasping my initial concept and for her sensitivity when things changed. To Elaine Lipson, for her thoughtfulness, wisdom, and guidance. To Michelle Bredeson, for her patience and skill in keeping the runaway train on track. To Linda Griepentrog, for making sure my math wasn't entirely imaginary. Thanks to the rest of the editorial and production teams for the countless things you do between concept and printed product, and to Julia Boyles, Joe Hancock, Missy Shepler, and the rest of the visual team for setting the look. Thanks also to Tricia Waddell and Amber Eden for opening so many doors.

To my local quilting friends, the Tuleburg Quilt Guild, and especially Helen Tellyer, Sandy Vieira, and Sandra Mollon, thanks for all your personal and professional support—and for being so welcoming when a twenty-something guy turned up out of the blue at a quilt guild!

Thanks to my parents, Bruce and Heather Kosbab, for imparting a creative drive in me and encouraging me to follow it wherever it led, and especially to my mom, who not only gave me a love of appliqué but also quilted several of the projects in the book. And to my husband, John Lessard: Neither I nor this book would be here without your endless well of encouragement and empathy, from which I drew so heavily during this long project.

index

Enjoy more quilting and sewing with these

top-notch resources

from Interweave

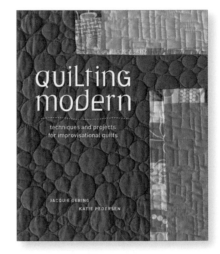

Stitch Workshop DVD: Secrets of Home Décor Sewing
Pillows, Cording, &
Simple Patchwork Slipcovers

Kevin Kosbab

ISBN 978-1-59668-763-9, $19.95

Quilting Modern
Techniques and Projects for
Improvisational Quilts

Jacquie Gering and Katie Pedersen

ISBN 978-1-59668-387-7, $26.95

Fresh Quilting
Fearless Color,
Design & Inspiration

Malka Dubrawsky

ISBN 978-1-59668-235-1, $26.95

▷ Available at your favorite retailer or **sew**daily shop shop.sewdaily.com ◁

stitch
CREATING WITH FABRIC + THREAD

Stitch magazine is all about creating with fabric and thread. Offering a fresh perspective on sewing, it's loaded with clever projects and modern designs. Find trendy and classic step-by-step projects, chats with inspiring designers, and the latest in sewing notions, fabrics, and patterns. Interweavestitch.com

sewdaily

Sew Daily is the ultimate online community for sewing enthusiasts. Get e-newsletters, download free articles and eBooks, discover tips and tricks from the experts, and find general all-around sewing information! Sign up at sewdaily.com.